Leonard Bernstein

A BIOGRAPHY FOR YOUNG PEOPLE

OTHER BOOKS BY DAVID EWEN

The World of Jerome Kern: A Biography

Complete Book of the American Musical Theater

Richard Rodgers

A Journey to Greatness: The Life and Music of George Gershwin

The Encyclopedia of the Opera

The Encyclopedia of Concert Music

A Panorama of American Popular Music

The Home Book of Musical Knowledge

Milton Cross' Encyclopedia of Great Composers and Their Music
(with Milton Cross)

The Complete Book of 20th Century Music

Music for the Millions

Dictators of the Baton

Music Comes to America

The Book of Modern Composers

BIOGRAPHIES FOR YOUNG PEOPLE

The Story of George Gershwin

The Story of Irving Berlin

The Story of Jerome Kern

Haydn: A Good Life

Tales from the Vienna Woods: The Story of Johann Strauss

The Story of Arturo Toscanini

Leonard Bernstein

A BIOGRAPHY FOR YOUNG PEOPLE

David Ewen, 1907-

*"All music is creation. It is one of the most
mysterious and deeply moving experiences
you can have."*—LEONARD BERNSTEIN

CHILTON COMPANY — BOOK DIVISION
PUBLISHERS   PHILADELPHIA AND NEW YORK

Contents

PRELUDE: *"One Sunday Afternoon"* 1

PART ONE: *"The Winter of Discontent"* 7
  1 "I Was a Miserable, Terrified Little Child" . . 7
  2 "I Knew with Finality I Would Be a Musician" . 12
  3 "It Was as Though I Didn't Exist Without Music" 17
  4 "One of the Most Mysterious and Deeply Moving Experiences" 23
  5 "There Was No Place for Me" 30
  6 "It Seemed the Most Natural Thing in the World for Me to Be Conducting" 34
  7 "This Was My Valley Forge" 44
  8 "Here We Go!" 53

ENTR'ACTE 1: *"Why Is a Conductor Necessary?"* . . 59

PART TWO: *"Made Glorious Summer by This Sun . . ."* . 67
  9 "I Live in a Schizophrenic World" . . . 67
  10 "Lenny" 78
  11 "An Artist Has the Compulsion to Work" . . 84
  12 "When I'm Conducting, Nothing Else Exists" . 91
  13 "The Only Way One Can Really Say Anything About Music Is to Write Music" 101
  14 "The Happy Medium" 113
  15 "Who Do I Think I Am—Everybody?" . . . 120

v

ENTR'ACTE II: *"The History of the Philharmonic Is the History of Music in America"* 129

PART THREE: *"And All the Clouds That Lour'd upon Our House in the Deep Bosom of the Ocean Buried"* 133

16 "What an Orchestra!—I Am a Happy Man" . . 133
17 "Audiences Are the Same the World Over" . . 139

CODA: *"Whither Lenny?"* 151

APPENDIX

I Works by Leonard Bernstein 157
II Recordings of Leonard Bernstein's Music . . . 163
III About Leonard Bernstein 165

INDEX 167

Leonard Bernstein

A BIOGRAPHY FOR YOUNG PEOPLE

"One Sunday Afternoon"

It hardly seemed likely that the big news on that Sunday afternoon of November 14, 1943, would come out of Carnegie Hall.

The world was at war. In every combat area—from the mud of southern Italy to the vast expanses of the Soviet Union and across the jungles of the Pacific—the forces of the free world were locked in a life-and-death struggle with a formidable enemy. But by November 1943 the tide of war had finally turned, implacably if still slowly, in our favor. In the Soviet Union, where Kiev had just been retaken by the Red Army, the Nazi hordes were in retreat. In Africa, the sad remnants of a once proud, conquering Nazi army had been trapped on Cape Bon; to all intents and purposes the war there was over. General Douglas MacArthur's troops landed successfully on New Guinea, while those of General Mark Clark had finally made the first penetration into fortress Europe at Salerno, Italy.

Surely, if some piece of news would arrest the interest and the excitement of the American people when they opened their favorite newspaper on Monday morning, November 15, it would come out of some field of battle.

Perhaps the story would tell of a new rousing victory, perhaps of another strategic advance, perhaps of a new invasion, perhaps of a further portent of our ultimate victory. Yet the news that captured most Americans that Monday morning was not of war but of peace; not of death and destruction but of life and the creation of music. Of all the dramatic, grim, heroic, soul-searing episodes that must have taken place all over the face of the globe on that Sunday afternoon, the biggest piece of news proved to be a symphony concert.

Nor, as they filed into Carnegie Hall, could subscribers to the New York Philharmonic that day have suspected that something special was about to take place. The concert that afternoon followed traditional grooves, not much different from hundreds of others that had taken place on earlier Sundays. The conductor was no stranger: he was the venerable Bruno Walter, come to make one of his many guest appearances with this orchestra. The program was not unusual. Except for a single world première (and that one, by a comparatively unknown composer, hardly calculated to arouse much anticipation) it was made up of familiar items by Schumann, Richard Strauss, and Wagner.

But what the Philharmonic audience in the hall (and the radio public throughout the country) did not know until concert time was that Bruno Walter was sick in bed and that a last-minute substitute had been called in hurriedly. This replacement was no familiar veteran of the baton. He was a young American of twenty-five named Leonard Bernstein, who had just that season been appointed assistant conductor of the Philharmonic.

Inside Carnegie Hall, the audience saw a strikingly handsome youth—looking more like a college undergraduate than a full-fledged maestro—stride vigorously, if also somewhat self-consciously, across the stage. He was wearing an ordinary gray business suit instead of formal attire. There was no baton in his hand as he lifted it over the orchestra for the first down-beat. He presented a picture of informality, almost as though he were about to direct a high-school orchestra in an assembly instead of one of the world's greatest orchestras in one of the world's most renowned concert auditoriums.

The opening three chords of Schumann's *Manfred Overture* pierced sharply through and shattered the expectant hush that had flooded the hall. The young man's supple, expressive hands seemed to shape the tones in midair as if they were a piece of clay being molded into a statue. As the overture progressed he revealed himself as a musician who knew what he was about. The beat was efficient, exact, precise. The cupped hand vibrated eloquently near his heart. The graceful motions of both hands continually suggested changing shades of color and nuances. Here was a conductor who, as the saying goes, did not have his head in the score but the score in his head. He hardly glanced at the printed page before him. Indeed, his eyes were closed; the mobile, eloquent face reflected sensitively all the moods and emotions of the music; the body moved with suppleness.

Not a moment of doubt, not a suggestion of uncertainty or confusion entered into his conducting for the remainder of that program. He seemed to know precisely what he wanted, both from the music and the musicians, and his demands were ful-filled almost as if in reflex action. It did not take long for that audience in Carnegie Hall (or the nationwide radio public either) to recognize that they were in the presence of that *rara avis* in music, a "born conductor." This young man knew his scores, could completely dominate the musicians under him, and was able to charge the atmosphere about him with magnetic sparks and transmit currents of electricity throughout the audi-torium.

When the concert ended, the *cognoscenti* gathered in little groups outside Carnegie Hall. Some lingered on for a while in the street. Some gathered for cocktails at the Russian Tea Room a few doors down. Some dropped in for a cup of coffee in the drugstore on the corner. All the talk everywhere in or about Carnegie Hall seemed to concentrate on the exciting youngster who had just made such an impressive debut. By now the word had circulated swiftly that before that day Bernstein had never conducted a major orchestra. More wonderful still, he had directed the exacting program of that afternoon on less than twenty-four hours' notice, without the benefit of a single rehearsal! Some people surmised that probably he was the youngest man ever to direct the Philharmonic, which actually was the case. Others, in a somewhat more flippant mood, remarked that another fact had set this concert in a class by itself: surely nobody before had led the august Philharmonic dressed in a business suit!

Veteran concertgoers hunted the storehouse of their memories for another conducting debut as dramatic, exciting, and unprecedented as this one had been. They could come up with only one: the time the awesome Arturo Toscanini, the greatest conductor of the 20th century, made his own bow. This event took place in Rio de Janeiro, in South America. A visiting Italian company was giving there a spring season of opera performances. On June 25, 1886, the regular conductor, because of differences with the management, defected from his scheduled appearance in *Aida*. At curtain time a nineteen-year-old cellist in the opera orchestra, Arturo Toscanini, was asked by the directors of the company to take over the baton. This young Italian had never before conducted any kind of performance anywhere. But it was general knowledge in the company that he possessed a fabulous memory, extraordinary ear, and profound musicianship. The feeling was that he might very well be able to conduct the performance that evening without blunders or mishaps. The young Toscanini went to the stand with his head bent and baton slung under his armpit. Without even opening the score on the desk before him, he proceeded

4

to direct from memory a performance of *Aida* such as had never before been given by that company, or for that matter such as Rio de Janeiro had previously heard—authoritatively, electrically. When the opera ended, a thunderous ovation acclaimed him. The career of one of the world's greatest conductors had begun.

The striking parallel between Toscanini and Bernstein did not escape some of those who gathered after the concert. Both men had made their debuts without any previous experience, and both men had given commanding performances without a single rehearsal. An inevitable question haunted many that day. Had they just witnessed the historic beginnings of *another* Toscanini?

Apparently some of the newspapers thought so. The next morning the New York critics lauded Bernstein's performance without reservation, in one or two cases these notices appeared on the front page. There was even comment in many editorial columns. Syndicates spread the story of the debut to newspapers, large and small, in every part of the country. Completely unknown only twenty-four hours earlier, Bernstein awoke on Monday morning to find he was famous.

He was an "overnight success," a term frequently found in biographies of musicians and actors and playwrights. But in music, as elsewhere, many an "overnight success" comes only after years of struggle, frustration, perhaps even despair.

Young though he was when he first became famous, Leonard Bernstein had been no exception.

PART ONE

"*The Winter of Discontent*"

"I was a miserable, terrified little child"

The history of music tells many a story of parents driving their sons to music study relentlessly, at times with extreme cruelty. Such was the case with Beethoven's father. Music history also abounds with tales of other parents—let us say the fathers of Handel, Schumann, and Johann Strauss II— who were equally severe and despotic in trying to keep their sons away from music.

Leonard Bernstein belongs to the latter group. One day in the summer of 1956, after Bernstein had brilliantly conducted a concert at Tanglewood, his father remarked sadly: "Every genius had a handicap. Lenny had a father."

Lenny's father is Samuel Joseph Bernstein—a successful businessman who from the beginning was determined to have

Lenny engage in the world of commerce rather than of art. As the son of a Chassidic scholar, Samuel Bernstein had in his native Russia been steeped in religious lore; thus he was well able to appreciate spiritual values over material ones. Indeed, from the time Lenny was a child, Samuel made a conscious and studied effort to instill in the boy what the father described as "the godly spirit" (*"Ruach Elohim"*)—through religion, education, and an appreciation of life's nobler pursuits. As Samuel Bernstein liked to say: "Without such a spirit, a man is nothing, and the food in his mouth is like straw. With it, he is everything. He does not become dizzy when he reaches high places."

But in Samuel's estimation this godly spirit did not embrace music. In the Russian ghetto, where the older Bernstein had been raised, a musician was a *"klesmer"*—a humble, impoverished fellow. He played at weddings, parties, and sometimes even in public parks and squares. The living he was able to eke out from such performances made possible only a hand-to-mouth existence at best, while at worst it brought the most abject poverty. Samuel had known too many *klesmer* in Russia not to have acquired an instinctive revulsion to a profession that offered so little materially to its practitioners. And he had too long known the galling taste of poverty, the humiliation and degradation it inflicts on its victims, not to be in perpetual horror of it. No!—he would most certainly never permit any child of his to become a *klesmer!*

Like so many of his compatriots, Samuel Bernstein had come to America to find a refuge from the ghettos and pogroms of his native Russia. The year was approximately 1909, and he was about sixteen at the time. Also, like many of his compatriots, he settled in the slums of New York's East Side, where he soon found a job cleaning fish beneath the Brooklyn Bridge. For this work his only compensation were the pennies grateful customers would drop into a tin box as a tip, usually amounting

8

to about a dollar a day. Such an income could permit him to live only in a dark, dank, airless room of a congested tenement, and to allow him only a few cents a day for food, which generally consisted of nothing more than a slice of black bread and some herring.

Samuel was an ambitious lad. After his day's work he would go to evening school to learn the language of his new homeland. He was ever on the lookout for ways in which to better himself. When he was nineteen he took a civil service examination which he failed because of imperfect spelling. Soon after that he became an errand boy for a beauty-parlor supply firm. When this shop opened a branch in Boston he was able to convince the owner to send him there as its manager. In Boston he married Jennie Resnick, also a native of Russia. He also managed through hard work, indefatigable drive, and initiative to save enough money to buy out the store where he was employed and set out for himself as a supplier to beauty parlors and barber shops, and in time to make the Samuel J. Bernstein Hair Supplies Company a thriving business.

His first child was Leonard—born in Lawrence, Massachusetts, on August 25, 1918. At the time the Bernsteins were living in Boston proper. They were vacationing with some relatives in Lawrence when the mother had her birth pangs and was rushed to its hospital where Lenny was born. A half dozen years later came Shirley. With the birth of Burton in 1931 the immediate family circle was completed.

During Lenny's childhood and boyhood, his family frequently changed residence in or near Boston. To find himself continually in a new neighborhood—with ever unfamiliar points of reference and among boys who were strangers—would have proved an emotionally disturbing experience even for a normal boy. And Lenny was no normal boy. From birth on he had been a victim of chronic asthma, of rose fever, of hay fever. He was continually taken to doctors, continually given injections. He became a sickly, skinny, unhappy little boy who did not make friends easily. He was in perpetual terror of the neighborhood boys because he was usually the helpless victim of their aggressions. Lenny, consequently, became an introvert. He preferred the security of his home to the society of friends or the diversion of kids' games. In addition, his parents' continual concern over his health, well-being, and even his appearance (which they did not try to hide from him) served to aggravate his stifling sense of inferiority. He became a sad, lonely, maladjusted boy, whose major concern was to be left strictly alone.

Since neither parent was musical, there was little good music in the Bernstein household. A phonograph was a part of the living-room furniture, but the only pieces of music Lenny remembers hearing on it were the hit songs of the day, such as "Barney Google" and "Oh, by Jingo!" Nevertheless, a few musical experiences managed to touch him. When they did the effect on him was far-reaching. He was about eight years old when his father took him one Saturday morning to the local synagogue, where the music of the organ and the choir made the boy burst into tears. At about the same time, while visiting relatives or friends who owned pianos, he would always drift away from their company to find his way to the keyboard where he would immediately become totally absorbed in the game of combining random tones into familiar tunes.

Then, one magic day he has never forgotten, he came home from his religious classes at the Temple Mishkan Tefila, to find a piano standing in his own living room. His Aunt Clara had sent it over to his house for temporary storage. It was an old, weatherbeaten, ugly upright instrument. But to the eleven-year-old boy it was a thing of ineffable beauty. "I made love to it right away," he recalls, by trying to play on it the melodies he knew to his own improvised accompaniments, songs like Irving Berlin's "Blue Skies."

A new world now opened up for Lenny. It was the first

10

world where he could be completely at ease; where he could find solace, joy, and stimulation; where the problems and harassments of his everyday life did not exist. The moment he came home from school he would rush to the piano. He would stay there for hours at an end. His sister, Shirley, recalls more than one evening during her childhood when she was kept awake by the sounds of Lenny's musical tinkerings. Late one night the entire family was awakened by the piano. The father stumbled into the living room and shouted: "Lenny, don't you know what time it is? It's two o'clock! What in heaven's name are you doing?" Lenny answered firmly: "I have to do this. The sounds are in my head and I have to get them out."

Like the proverbial love affair, this one with the piano refused to run a smooth course. Lenny's parents had long since decided that he would be the one, someday, to take over the already flourishing beauty-supply business. They wanted nothing to frustrate these plans. Every time Lenny was at the piano, they would nag him to leave it alone and do his homework instead. They argued, and at times they became explosively angry. But Lenny stubbornly refused to surrender his precious hours with music.

"I knew with finality," he has said, "I would be a musician."

CHAPTER 2

"I knew with finality I would be a musician"

After the piano had been in the Bernstein living room about a month, Lenny began asking for lessons. Even iron must melt in the presence of intense heat. Lenny's parents, faced by his intransigeance, were finally compelled to relent and allow him to seek out a teacher. Scouting the neighborhood, he came upon a woman in the vicinity who charged $1.00 a lesson. She taught him for about two years, feeding him on "The Mountain Belle" and "On to Victory," and similar trifles which he performed at her annual students concerts. When she married and moved to California, Lenny acquired a teacher in downtown Boston whose fee was $3.00 a lesson. This increase in price represented a major crisis in the Bernstein household, for Lenny's father stubbornly refused to pay the price for the lessons. A compromise was worked out in which Lenny gave up all but 25 cents of his allowance while his father paid the piano teacher.

This second period of study, lasting a little over a year, almost proved a disaster for Lenny. His teacher had a method which required the hands to be held rigidly, knuckles down, while the fingers moved stiffly across the keys. Subjecting himself to such taxing and unnatural digital discipline could have permanently damaged the muscles of the hands if fortunately

—perhaps from an instinctive feeling for self-preservation—Lenny had not suddenly decided to seek out a new teacher. At this crucial period in his training, he was able to find the *right* teacher.

One of the most distinguished instructors of the piano in Boston was Heinrich Gebhard. He was then fifty-two, behind him a distinguished career as concert pianist (begun in 1896) which placed him in the front rank of interpreters of Impressionist music. Lenny, determined to get the best possible instruction available in Boston—and made fully aware of the remarkable background and reputation of this teacher—asked for and received an audition. Bernstein played a few of the compositions he had recently learned—and in the unnatural position of hands which he had been taught. Gebhard smiled sadly, and told the boy as gently as he could that he was not yet ready for whatever Gebhard could offer him. "A few years from now, perhaps—we shall see. But not yet, my boy, not yet." Gebhard, however, came up with a valuable suggestion: Why not study with Gebhard's competent assistant, a young lady named Helen Coates? She was eminently qualified to teach the boy. If he made favorable progress with her, he could then begin studying with Gebhard. There was also another, and highly practical, reason why, for the time being, Helen Coates was preferable to Gebhard where Lenny was concerned. Gebhard received $25.00 a lesson, a sum Bernstein knew he would never be able to raise. Helen Coates was willing to take him on for $6.00 a lesson, a price Lenny could cope with by taking only one lesson every two weeks.

Helen Coates immediately set about the serious business of repairing the damage inflicted on Lenny by his previous teacher. He was subjected to a rigorous diet of scales, exercises, and etudes by Czerny, Chopin, and others. But Helen Coates was not a martinet concerned merely with the position of hands, wrists, and fingers, important though she regarded such instruction. She was a sensitive musician and a sympathetic and compassionate human being well able to understand and respond to a student like Lenny. When she discovered he had a seemingly insatiable appetite for music, she extended his musical diet to a lavish full-course meal. She encouraged him to listen to performances of good music on the radio; she advised him to borrow musical scores from the library and learn to read them as one might a novel; she took a personal interest in the music he himself was already trying to write. Recognizing in Bernstein an alert, restless, and expansive intelligence, she did not hesitate to have him discuss with her whatever was on his mind at any given moment—not only music but also poetry or politics or good books.

"He used to come to me right from school," she says. "Since I never knew when he'd go home, I never scheduled anyone after him. He'd bring me his report cards, poems, questions on world topics. He talked about everything."

The one-hour lesson soon overflowed into an hour and a half, then into two hours. Lenny brought to Helen Coates' studio some of the scores he borrowed from the library, and teacher and pupil would go through them at the piano. While rummaging among the shelves of published music in the library, Bernstein came upon opera, up to that time for him *terra incognita*. He would divide the principal roles with Helen Coates, and they would plow through entire scenes. (He did the same thing at home. Shirley, now aged nine, would sing the female parts, and Lenny the male, both making desperate attempts to pronounce the French, Italian, or German words, even though at the time neither one had any knowledge of these languages.) Lenny would also show Coates some of his compositions, sometimes popular tunes, sometimes highly ambitious works. One day he brought her a piano concerto in a romantic style which he had written before he had begun taking lessons with her—music so derivative of Tschaikovsky and Liszt that he later described it facetiously as "a tug of war between the Russians and the gypsies."

"He was frighteningly gifted," recalls Helen Coates. "He could read, sing, and memorize anything. He absorbed in one lesson an arrangement that took most of my pupils five or six lessons to learn."

To Bernstein's father, this passionate, seemingly irresistible, dedication to music on Lenny's part was a matter for deep concern. Nevertheless, he could not fail to notice the extraordinary change for the better beginning to take place with the boy. At the exacting Boston Latin School, which Lenny had entered in his eleventh year after attending neighborhood grammar schools, he was a brilliant all-around student. He was also outstanding in his religious studies at Temple Mishkan Tefila, where for his Confirmation he wrote his own speech, a brilliant one in the Hebrew tongue. It was almost as if his musical training had become a whetstone on which he had sharpened his intelligence to a keen edge. But this was not all that music had done for him. A remarkable transformation was taking place even in his physical and personal make-up. Apparently music had proved the stimulus he needed to change a sickly, pitiable little boy into a well-built, vigorous athlete; to transform a retiring and self-conscious misfit into a well-poised social being. Bernstein himself put it this way: "One day I was a scrawny little thing that everybody could beat up, and the next time I looked around I was the biggest boy in class. I could run faster, jump higher, dive better than anybody." At a summer camp in 1932 he won first prize in high jumping and proved adept at swimming, diving, and horseback riding. He was also now for the first time extremely popular—especially when he entertained boys with his renditions at the piano of Tin Pan Alley tunes and jazz. These impromptu little performances—supplemented by concerts in the school auditorium and appearances as soloist with the Boston Public School

Orchestra—helped make out of him an extrovert who took inordinate delight in sharing his own musical experiences with others. He no longer hesitated to accept invitations to parties. On the contrary, he now began to seek them out eagerly. There was hardly a party where he did not become a focal point of interest. "I just ran for the piano as soon as I got in the door and stayed there until they threw me out. It was as though I didn't exist without music."

CHAPTER 3

"It was as though I didn't exist without music"

Lenny was engaged in music all the time, at the slightest provocation. When he was not playing the piano he was reading musical scores borrowed from the Newton library with the same open-eyed fascination with which other boys devoured science fiction or books about sports. His neighbors regarded him as an eccentric because while walking to and from the library—or to and from school—he would often nod to himself, chuckle, grimace while reading the music. "I can hear it in my head as I read it," he confided to a friend.

Again and again he provided testimony to his singular passion for every kind and type of music. He spent several summers at a boys' camp in Sharon, Massachusetts. Though by now an adept athlete who freely participated in several different forms of sport, his happiest hours came from helping to produce, write, and direct the camp shows. For one of these performances he prepared a burlesque of Bizet's opera *Carmen*, casting himself as the seductive gypsy cigarette girl! At other times he offered condensed versions of the more popular Gilbert and Sullivan comic operas. He managed to inveigle his father into providing the cast with wigs, and for a production of *Pinafore* he even prevailed on his mother to allow the housemaid, Leila, to appear in the cast. One year he recruited his sister, Shirley, to play Yum-Yum in *The Mikado.*

Already his capacity to arouse the interest of those around him in his musicmaking was exceptional. Soon after his thirteenth birthday, his father took him on a cruise through the Panama Canal. Aboard ship his piano music proved such a continual source of entertainment that the cruise director tried to get him to join his permanent staff. At another time, on a brief vacation in Florida, he once again was the center of interest with his lively piano playing. Even his father—opposed though he was to Lenny's preoccupation with music—began recruiting the boy to entertain at parties of business organizations or fraternal orders. Lenny's repertory consisted of pop tunes, show tunes, jazz, the classics—topped off with what for a long time was his *tour de force,* an original melody played in the styles of many different composers from Bach and Mozart to Gershwin.

In the summer of 1933, a Boston newspaper sponsored a music-information contest in which first prize was a baby-grand piano. The rules specified that contestants be sixteen years or older. Lenny was still a year from that minimum-age requirement but the promise of at last owning a baby-grand piano proved too enticing to be resisted. He entered the competition, falsifying his age on the entry blank. For weeks after that his conscience was tortured by this fraud, and at one of his piano lessons he broke down and confessed his guilt to his teacher. As it turned out he did not win the piano, being only the runner-up. His prize was a set of worthless piano music— third-rate pieces and poor transcriptions—which Lenny dumped with disgust.

Musical experiences soon began to accumulate. He attended his first concert in 1934, a performance by Serge Rachmaninoff at Symphony Hall. Exciting though this event was—and he still remembers each detail of Rachmaninoff's piano playing— he heard another concert that same year, though this time on the radio, which stirred him to his very marrow, and opened up new vistas of musical appreciation. This was a broadcast by the Boston Symphony conducted by Serge Koussevitzky, whose program included Serge Prokofiev's *Classical Symphony* and Igor Stravinsky's *The Rite of Spring*. This was Lenny's initiation into modern music. A brave new world of musical sound and experience stunned his senses and dazzled his imagination. "Until then," he says, "I never realized that music had a future. I always thought of it as something that had already been written." The witty unexpected leaps in melody, whimsical change of key, incongruous juxtaposition of tart harmonies and classical ones in the Prokofiev symphony made Lenny laugh out loud until his eyes smarted with tears and his chest ached with stabbing pains. After that came the searing dissonances and the primitive rhythms of Stravinsky's music. A strange kind of excitement, a kind of inner frenzy, seized and held Lenny.

He now began to seek out other scores by Stravinsky and Prokofiev, studied them, memorized them, grew to love them. The impact of this music on his development was immediately reflected as he went on to write a piano sonata in an *avant-garde* style.

He started attending performances of the Boston Symphony at Symphony Hall more or less regularly, sometimes on a date. One evening the conductor, Serge Koussevitzky, received an ovation for a particularly stirring performance. Lenny remained silent and glum in his seat. His girl friend asked him if he had not liked the way Koussevitzky had played that particular work. "Not like it?" he replied hotly. "I *loved* it! That's the trouble. I'm just jealous of any man who can make that kind of music."

This intense, feverish preoccupation with music; this continual excitement from making ever new discoveries among composers and compositions; this wonderful feeling of self-fulfillment from acquiring skill in playing the piano, reading a score, and putting musical thoughts down on paper—all this might have spelled for Lenny a happy boyhood. Regrettably this was not the case. Within himself there might be complete harmony, but in his adjustment to his parents as far as music was concerned there was only discord. They were becoming increasingly concerned over the way music was dominating his life, habits, thoughts, interests. His father did not hesitate to speak his mind. Bitter arguments between him and Lenny became the rule of the household.

Again and again, and with considerable heat, the father would insist that all this nonsense with music must be curtailed if not altogether stopped. Lenny, he insisted, must think seriously of finishing his schoolwork with flying colors, proceed to an outstanding college, and later on enter the family business. Lenny was no less vehement that he would never go into any business, that nothing and no one could stand in his way of becoming a musician.

A *musician*? "What kind of a future is that for a sensible young man?" the father would ask in anguish. Did Lenny want to become one of those sad, harassed piano teachers whose life's mission was to drill recalcitrant pupils in scales and exercises for $1.00 or $2.00 a lesson? Did he aspire to play hack music with some hotel orchestra or jazz ensemble? Or did his ambition embrace the writing of esoteric music—something like that crazy-sounding piano sonata he had just finished—music nobody heard and nobody played? "Oh, yes!"—the father would continue to press his arguments—"it's all very fine if you are a Koussevitzky, a Toscanini, a Heifetz, or a Rachmaninoff. I know these men do very well for themselves. But how many Koussevitzkys, Toscaninis, Heifetzes, or Rachmaninoffs are there around anyway?" Did Lenny, even in his wildest dreams, think he was one of them? Except for the immortals, summed up the father, a professional career in music invited only a lifetime of frustration, bitterness, futility, and suffering.

And so, from one evening to another, the father tried argument, persuasion, entreaty, orders, and anger to deflect Lenny from his music. When these failed he turned to more positive action. On one occasion he sternly announced he was discontinuing Lenny's allowance so that there might no longer be any money for piano lessons. But this strategy failed. Lenny went on to find a job after school hours playing the piano in a jazz band and thus earned enough to pay his teacher. After that, the father wrote long, appealing letters to Helen Coates to do what she could to discourage the boy's absorption with music. But Helen Coates refused to be a partner to such a conspiracy and turned a deaf ear to these entreaties. By now she was not only convinced of Lenny's immense talent and potential but also of the complete futility of trying to arrest the oceanic surge of his enthusiasm for music.

After Lenny had become world-famous, his father insisted to an interviewer that it was not so much from music study that he had tried so hard to keep his son as from trying to make a living out of music. "From the early 16th century, my family never made a livelihood in art, and I didn't want to break this tradition," he said. "I also felt Lenny could make a better living in business. Remember there was no Leonard Bernstein then. There might not be another Leonard Bernstein for a thousand years. I'm very proud of Lenny, but the Talmud teaches us, 'Don't expect miracles.' Because God blessed the world with a Leonard Bernstein, it doesn't mean his parents should expect it. You don't *expect* your child to be a Moses, a Maimonides, a Leonard Bernstein. If I had to do it all over again, I'd do the same thing."

In 1935, Lenny was graduated from the Boston Latin School with honors. In academic achievement he was in the top ten per cent of his class. In his musical accomplishment he was alone, for he was the proud composer of the graduating-class song. The next stop was Harvard. A truce had finally been effected between father and son. The former promised that, for the time being, he would adopt a *laissez-faire* policy toward Lenny's music on the condition that Lenny continued doing well with his schoolwork at Harvard. A final decision about his future—whether in business or in music—could wait until he had completed college. However, if Lenny still wanted to continue his piano study, he would have to find the money for his lessons himself. Lenny found that money by teaching children the piano for $1.00 an hour. In one special case, where the family had three children studying the piano, he accepted them for $2.00 a lesson with supper thrown in for good measure.

CHAPTER 4

"One of the most mysterious and deeply moving experiences"

The four years at Harvard were filled with music. Some of Lenny's fellow students used to remark wryly that at times no note of music was sounded anywhere in Cambridge without his having had some share in its making.

In the classroom he was always a good, and at times a brilliant, student—brilliant in languages, philosophy, and music. His music study at Harvard embraced counterpoint and theory (his first formal training in these subjects) and music history with professors such as Walter Piston, Arthur Tillman Merritt, and Edward Burlingame Hill.

Extracurricular musical activities were many and varied. He had passed from Helen Coates' fastidious and extremely valuable piano instruction to that of Heinrich Gebhard, who now subjected him to a severe, but to Bernstein's tastes a highly palatable, diet of modern music, including such taxing works as Ravel's G major Piano Concerto (later to become one of Bernstein's particular specialities as pianist-conductor) and Aaron Copland's *Piano Variations*. Though Bernstein's ambition at the time was the concert stage, he was not neglecting creative work; in 1936 he completed some smaller pieces for the piano.

Where there was music, there, too, was Lenny. He appeared as soloist with both the college orchestra and the Massachusetts State Orchestra, the latter a WPA organization giving concerts in Cambridge. He was piano accompanist for the college glee club. He wrote music, helped stage, and performed in, several College Day japes. He was the pianist for programs of silent motion pictures presented by a student film club.

Those silent-film piano accompaniments made a profound impression on those who heard them, both for Bernstein's already remarkable technical facility and for his extraordinary and unorthodox choice of compositions. Irving Fine, now himself a distinguished American composer but in the late 1930's Bernstein's fellow student at Harvard, recalled in *Modern Music:* "I remember with great nostalgia his appearance as piano accompanist at a series of historical films presented by the Harvard Film Society. *The Battleship Potemkin* rode at anchor to the accompaniment of Copland's *Piano Variations,* excerpts from Stravinsky's *Petrouchka,* and Bernstein's own paraphrases of Russian folk songs."

As a member of the Harvard Music Club, Bernstein gave frequent performances at its concerts. Sometimes he was called on at the last moment to substitute for a young artist unable to make his scheduled appearance. "Many . . . programs," adds Irving Fine, "would have been lost if Bernstein had not been willing to tackle, almost at sight, anything from the Stravinsky Concerto for Two Solo Pianos to a work by one of his fellow students. At these club meetings he performed some of his own earlier essays."

As if these activities were not enough to absorb his seemingly indefatigable energies, he was also writing music criticisms. His earliest piece of critical writing appeared in *The Advocate,* a college literary magazine for which he reviewed a Boston Symphony concert conducted by Koussevitzky. In 1938–1939, Bernstein also contributed reports to *Modern Music,* a quarterly review published in New York as the organ of the League of Composers. "Dr. Koussevitzky," he wrote in one of these pieces, "has had a great festival of brand new American works right at the fifty-yard line of the season." Apparently Bernstein's later flair for combining musical comment and analysis with the figures-of-speech of an undergraduate is already in evidence!

Even in summer, away from Harvard, Bernstein continued making music. Some were spent at Onota, where his main job was to put on stage productions. At times he was called on to perform sundry other musical duties as well. One day in 1937 the management asked Bernstein to provide the musical background at the piano during dinner on Visitors Day. After the parents had filed into the dining room and were about to partake of their meal, Bernstein quietly announced from his piano: "Ladies and gentlemen. This summer a great American composer died—George Gershwin. Let's pay him the tribute of not talking or eating, but just listening reverently to one of his compositions." Bernstein then played the Piano Concerto in F, oblivious to the embarrassment of the camp guests as they squirmed in front of a meal rapidly getting cold on the table! From then on, the project of having Bernstein play on Visitors Day was discreetly abandoned.

In his last year at Harvard, Bernstein was either a participant in or entirely responsible for two important musical events. One was a production of Aristophanes' *The Birds,* put on by the Harvard Classical Club, for which Bernstein wrote the incidental music. Upon the presentation of this Greek drama in Cambridge on April 21 and 22, 1939, Bernstein conducted the orchestra, his first such experience.

Even more ambitious was Bernstein's production of Marc Blitzstein's opera (or musical play) *The Cradle Will Rock.* This provocative social drama with music (for which Blitzstein wrote not only the music but also the text and lyrics) concerned attempts by steelworkers to create a union in a fictitious

American city, and the nefarious methods by which powerful business groups tried to stifle this undertaking. *The Cradle Will Rock* was first produced in New York in 1937 under dramatic and controversial circumstances. It was a production of the Federal Theater Project, supported by the U.S. Government. Because of the play's pronounced left-wing social viewpoints, it aroused considerable opposition in government circles who wanted the production banned. Just before the première performance, all support for the play was suddenly withdrawn in Washington. The right to use the costumes, the sets, and the orchestra was, consequently, denied. Rather than call off this performance, Orson Welles (the director) and John Houseman (the producer) decided to transfer the audience to a nearby theater and offer their play in oratorio style. The performers, dressed in their everyday clothes, were seated in several rows on the bare stage. When required to perform they stepped to the footlights. Marc Blitzstein, seated at the piano on the stage, played the score and made between-the-scene verbal comments on what was taking place.

Bernstein liked the play, and he was even more partial to Blitzstein's fresh, exciting marriage of popular tunes, parodies, and patter songs to sophisticated harmonic and contrapuntal approaches. When the Boston police refused permission for the performance of *The Cradle Will Rock* in that city, Bernstein decided to put it on exactly as it had been done in New York. The Boston constabulary could not interfere since Harvard was off-limits to them. Bernstein became director and co-ordinator of the whole production. He also took over Blitzstein's job of playing the music at the piano and making illuminating comments between the scenes. The performance proved an overwhelming success. The critics were rhapsodic both about the play and the performance, with Bernstein himself coming in for a lion's share of attention for his courage and initiative in having put on the production, and for the sound musical and dramatic values he brought to it.

This was Bernstein's first success as a performing musician. The sweet music of thunderous audience applause and singing praises of the critics convinced him that whatever his future in music might be, that future would have to be in the public eye, in communication with an audience. Reaching out to people through music, he later told an interviewer, was "one of the most mysterious and deeply moving experiences you can have." Now, on the eve of leaving both Harvard and his academic life, Bernstein knew decisively that it was toward such an experience that he must henceforth direct himself.

At Harvard, Bernstein came into personal contact with several musicians with whom he would henceforth maintain a close association. One was Marc Blitzstein, who had come to Boston to hear Bernstein's performance of *The Cradle Will Rock* and who was stunned by the authority and penetration of the young man's interpretation. They were drawn to each other not merely by a profound professional respect but also by their mutual interest in progressive social and political ideas. Again and again, later in his career, Bernstein would give striking performances of Blitzstein's music. When Bernstein's first child was born, Marc Blitzstein was its godfather.

Aaron Copland, sometimes described as the "dean of American composers," was another musician with whom Bernstein had personal associations at Harvard for the first time, and of whose music he subsequently became a most significant interpreter. Through a Harvard philosophy professor, a Copland admirer, Copland's music was brought to Bernstein's attention. Its immense technical skill and its freshness of musical thought and idiom impressed Bernstein deeply and immediately—so much so that he was now led to study the *Piano Variations* with

Gebhard. When Copland visited Harvard in 1937, a mutual acquaintance brought them together. They hit it off at once.

But of all the professional musicians encountered by Bernstein at college none had a more decisive impact on his future than Dimitri Mitropoulos. Mitropoulos was a Greek-born conductor who in 1935 had made a remarkable American debut as guest conductor of the Boston Symphony. In January 1937 he returned to Boston for more guest appearances. A tea was given in his honor one Sunday afternoon by the Harvard Hellenic Society at the Phillips Brook House. Bernstein had planned spending that day studying for his examinations, but when invited to meet Mitropoulos in the flesh his good intentions were nullified.

On arriving at the reception, Bernstein found the room overflowing with people, with Mitropoulos helplessly engulfed by a mass of admirers. For a long while Bernstein failed to approach him. But when some of the guests had departed, Bernstein was formally introduced to the conductor. They engaged at once in an extended conversation in which Bernstein told Mitropoulos of some of his musical interests and his hopes for the future. Mitropoulos then invited Bernstein to play for him. Bernstein performed a Chopin nocturne, and after that the last movement of his own piano sonata—"horribly" as he now recalls. But apparently Mitropoulos was impressed, for he invited Bernstein to attend his rehearsals with the Boston Symphony that week.

These were the first rehearsals by a great conductor attended by Bernstein, and they proved a cataclysmic experience. The hypnotic effect of conductor on orchestra; his penetrating insight into the music he was rehearsing; his immense musicianship and infallible taste—all this provided Bernstein for the first time with an understanding of the functions of a conductor. Bernstein now saw the conductor as he really was: a virtuoso of virtuosos; the supreme musical interpreter performing on the most complex musical instrument in the world, the symphony orchestra.

It is more than probable that, as Bernstein sat there in the empty, half-dark auditorium, it was now that he was fired for the first time with the ambition of becoming a conductor. If such a hope hovered for a while on the fringes of his subconscious, it did not remain there long. One day that week, while Bernstein was having lunch with Mitropoulos, the conductor playfully referred to him as a "genius boy" and seriously urged him to consider a career in conducting. This was the first time that such a suggestion was made to Bernstein. That it came from someone like Mitropoulos meant it could not be received lightly or readily dismissed from his thoughts.

What Bernstein saw and heard during those rehearsals had an effect on him far more profound and permanent than perhaps he suspects even now. One of the works Mitropoulos conducted was Schumann's Symphony No. 2 in C major. From the beginning of his professional career as conductor, Bernstein was partial to this masterwork and has performed it frequently. Another composition rehearsed by Mitropoulos was Malipiero's Piano Concerto, in which Mitropoulos himself was soloist, while conducting the accompaniment from the piano. Bernstein has also often filled the dual role of pianist-conductor. Finally, in his conducting Mitropoulos was given to extravagant gestures of body and hands. It is surely not beyond the realm of possibility that here, too, Bernstein was paying Mitropoulos that highest of all tributes, imitation, when in his own performances he indulged in similarly flamboyant mannerisms.

CHAPTER 5

"There was no place for me"

When Leonard Bernstein was graduated from Harvard with *cum laude* in music, in June 1939, he had good reason to have faith in his talent for music. He had repeatedly inspired nothing but the highest admiration and the most unqualified enthusiasm for his gifts: his extraordinary memory and ear; his facile ability to read even the most complex piece of music as if it were fiction; his aptitude at translating at the piano any opera or orchestral score; his articulateness in putting down on paper his musical thoughts. Dimitri Mitropoulos, Aaron Copland, Marc Blitzstein, William Schuman, Roy Harris, Walter Piston, Heinrich Gebhard—redoubtable musicians all of them!—were only a few of many who had prognosticated for him a most fruitful career in music.

Sure though he may have been of his musical endowments, he was far less confident of his purpose and direction. Whither Lenny? Now that his academic study had been completed—and with it his piano instruction with Heinrich Gebhard was terminated—he had to ask himself repeatedly: "Whither Lenny?" He had by now abandoned the dream of storming the citadels of Carnegie Hall as a piano virtuoso, and had begun to think of himself primarily as a composer. Yet nothing he had thus far written had either been published or performed in a formal concert auditorium. How, then, could he have any assurance that he could make a name for himself through his creative work? And even if he had such assurance, how could he possibly earn his living while waiting for recognition?

There had been a particularly stormy session at home soon after Lenny's graduation. His father offered to take him into his business and start him off at $100 a week. Lenny's immediate and unhesitating response was that he would not take the job if the salary were ten times that amount. He would never forget the time when, one dismal summer when he was sixteen, he had worked for about a month as shipping clerk in his father's establishment. Faced by Lenny's recalcitrance, the father made it perfectly plain that from this point on all financial support would be withdrawn.

Lenny knew he would have to brush the dust of Boston from his shoes, that now was the time for him to find a place for himself in New York's rich musical life.

He arrived in New York early that summer of 1939, in his pocket enough money to see him through for a few weeks. He found a cheap furnished room on East Ninth Street in an apartment occupied by two young men. One was Adolph Green, whom Bernstein first met one summer several years earlier at Camp Onota, to which Green had come as a visitor. At that time Bernstein had recruited Green to appear as the Pirate King in his production of the Gilbert and Sullivan comic opera, *The Pirates of Penzance*. They became fast friends. Bernstein liked Green's sharp intellect and ready gift for wit, satire, parody, and burlesque. And Green, himself a lover of good music, was in awe of Bernstein's talent.

On coming to New York, then, Adolph Green was one of the first persons Bernstein contacted, and Lenny was delighted to learn he could make his home in Green's apartment. In the summer of 1939, Green was working in a night-club act called "The Revuers"—one of its members being Betty Comden (later Green's successful collaborator in writing lyrics for songs and texts for musical comedies), and another, Judy Holliday (subsequently star of the Broadway stage and Hollywood screen). "The Revuers" was featured in a Greenwich Village night spot, *The Vanguard,* where they sang sophisticated songs written collaboratively by Green and Betty Comden.

Having found a place to live, Bernstein wasted no time in trying to find a job. This did not prove as easy as it had first appeared. To get any kind of employment as pianist he had to join the Musicians Union, and one of the requirements for membership was a six-months period of residence in New York. Without a job, Lenny decided to linger on in New York as long as his meager funds allowed. Perhaps something would turn up.

He was neither idle nor alone. On a few occasions he played the piano (without pay) for "The Revuers" at the Village *Vanguard.* They even made at the time a recording of a whimsical piece, "The Girl with Two Left Feet"—now a cherished collector's item. Many an evening Lenny could be found uptown in a twenty-five-cent seat at the Lewisohn Stadium, where symphony concerts were given under famous orchestras. Bernstein drank in the music, all the while allowing himself the luxury of lapsing into a euphoric state in which he envisioned himself as a professional musician performing before audiences. Some evenings were spent with Aaron Copland at Copland's apartment in stimulating conversations. Then there were the parties to which Green took Lenny, where Lenny helped entertain the guests at the piano. He delighted them particularly with the comical way in which, while playing the Ravel G major Piano Concerto in all seriousness, he would suddenly and unexpectedly shift to Irving Berlin's "Alexander's Ragtime Band." Late one night Betty Comden went home from one of these parties to awaken her mother and tell her about Bernstein's performance. "I met a *real* genius," she said excitedly. Harold Clurman, founder of the famous Group Theater in New York (nursery for such distinguished men of the stage as Clifford Odets, the playwright, Elia Kazan, the director, and John Garfield, the actor) was another who fell in love with Bernstein's informal performances. "Lenny," he would say, "is hopelessly fated for success."

Such a glowing prophecy surely must have had a hollow ring to a young man who saw his money disappearing rapidly without hope for replenishment, who could find no work anywhere. "There was just no place for me." For all the gay parties, for all the kind words of friends and acquaintances, the summer of 1939 was a period of sheer misery. He drifted into a state of depression. With just about enough money left to take him back to Boston, he was ready to concede defeat, to reconcile himself to the fact that he would have to work for his father if he were not to starve. "I went home with my tail between my knees."

CHAPTER 6

"It seemed the most natural thing in the world for me to be conducting"

Hardly had Bernstein returned to Boston when he heard from a friend that Dimitri Mitropoulos, en route to Europe, was at that moment stopping at the Biltmore Hotel in New York. Suddenly Mitropoulos represented to Bernstein his last hope for a career in music, his last avenue of escape from the business world he detested. Surely Mitropoulos, who in the past had been so encouraging, would find a way to help him! Lenny borrowed some money and took the first train back to New York. At the Biltmore he poured out his heart to Mitropoulos.

Mitropoulos agreed with Bernstein that to give up music was unthinkable, reaffirming his conviction that Bernstein had the makings of a fine conductor. But, Mitropoulos added, what Bernstein now needed was some specialized training. The veteran conductor stood ready to use his influence in getting an audition for him at the Curtis Institute of Music in Philadelphia, one of the country's most renowned music schools— even though enrollment for the coming semester was over. Mitropoulos was convinced that an intensive period of study with Fritz Reiner, the distinguished conductor—and one of

America's leading teachers of conducting—would give Bernstein that background and technique he would need to embark on a professional career with the baton. And Reiner was the head of the conducting department at Curtis. As for finances . . . Mitropoulos was sure that on his say-so Bernstein could get a scholarship. In addition, the conductor was willing to provide the young man with a small, but regular, stipend to help defray living expenses.

The week-end before his scheduled audition with Reiner at Curtis, Bernstein spent with Aaron Copland in the country, at Woodstock, New York. That brief holiday further boosted Lenny's morale, for Copland was as sure as Mitropolous had been that Bernstein would have no trouble in convincing Reiner to give him a scholarship; and also like Mitropoulos, Copland felt that Bernstein's forte in music lay in conducting. But that week-end proved far less beneficial to Bernstein's health. Ever victimized by his allergies, Bernstein left Woodstock for Philadelphia stricken by a severe attack brought on by contacts with Copland's household pet, a cat. Lenny arrived for his interview with Reiner not only tense with anxiety, but also with a swollen face and with fits of coughing and sneezing.

Fritz Reiner invited Bernstein to read at the piano, at sight, the orchestral score of Brahms' *Academic Festival Overture*. This proved such child's play for Lenny that Reiner was led to inquire if Bernstein had not previously studied that music thoroughly. Convinced that this performance had been unrehearsed, Reiner did not hesitate to accept Bernstein as his pupil and to arrange a scholarship for him.

Leonard Bernstein entered the Curtis Institute in the fall of 1939 and remained there until June 1941. Life now might often prove stimulating and exciting for Bernstein, but it was by no means easy. While he did not have to pay for tuition, nevertheless the meager allowance doled out to him permitted only the barest essentials of living. A small, stuffy furnished room in a boarding house was his home all the time he stayed in Philadelphia. Most of his meals were taken at nearby drugstore counters. There was no money for clothes, luxuries, or tickets to theater or concerts. His only diversion—apart from playing the piano and reading scores—came from visiting the studios of friends where impromptu parties blossomed on Saturday evenings and Sunday afternoons. Conversations and discussions were provocative. On Sundays they would often listen to the broadcasts of the New York Philharmonic and argue hotly the pros and cons of the music they had heard and of the way it was played. As heretofore, Bernstein was a prolific contributor to the gaiety of these social gatherings with his piano playing. What he now liked to do particularly was to present ridiculous little parodies of his own writing. He would sing them at the top of his voice to his own witty piano accompaniment—often breaking up his performances with his own fits of uncontrolled laughter.

Besides attending Reiner's conducting class, Bernstein studied piano with Isabella Vengerova. She was a tyrant who was impatient with Lenny's tendency at the time to lose himself so passionately and completely in the music he was playing that he often lost all objectivity and capacity for self-criticism. He was (truth to tell) often in terror of her strict regimen—so severe was she in her criticisms, so unrelenting in her discipline, so exacting in her demands on students. But Lenny did not hesitate to acknowledge that these lessons with Mme. Vengerova were the necessary finishing touches in making him a pianist of concert caliber.

Reiner's class in conducting was for Lenny an unadulterated joy. His first experience in conducting an orchestra (other than his performance at Harvard when he led his own music for Aristophanes' *The Birds*) came during his first term at Curtis. Reiner asked him to lead the Curtis Institute Orchestra in a performance of Randall Thompson's Second Symphony. At the time Thompson was not only an outstanding American composer but also the director of Curtis Institute, and Bernstein's teacher there in orchestration. "I was scared, tremendously scared," Bernstein recalls. But by the time he mounted the podium he knew the music so thoroughly that he could absorb himself completely with his performance, which delighted Thompson no end. Bernstein's reaction to this first important attempt at directing an orchestra was: "It then seemed the most natural thing in the world for me to be conducting."

One of Bernstein's assignments in Reiner's class was to prepare an orchestral composition of his own choosing for performance at the piano. For some unexplained reason he never quite got around to doing this exercise. On the day he was required to do this chore in class he rushed into the school library and hastily picked off the shelves the first available score—Beethoven's *Coriolanus Overture*. In class he dashed the music off at sight with such ease and musicianship that fellow students insisted he was "putting on an act," refusing to believe he had done this without preparation. Their skepticism and even antagonism were not completely dissipated until Bernstein was able to demonstrate time and again, during the next few months, how easy it was for him to read orchestral scores at the piano. Fritz Reiner, who described him as a "human gyroscope," went on to say that Lenny was "the most talented, all around student I ever had."

Each summer there took place one of America's most important music festivals in Lenox, Massachusetts, on the grounds of Tanglewood which had been the setting of Nathaniel Hawthorne's famous *Tanglewood Tales*. The annual Berkshire Symphonic Festival, as it was called, was dominated by the personality of Serge Koussevitzky, music director of the Boston Symphony. By this time Koussevitzky was something of a legend in music circles, by virtue of his genius as an interpreter of symphonic music, of his lifelong dedication to and sponsorship of modern music, and of his electrifying personality. He was the man who, after having become one of the world's foremost virtuosos on the double bass, had founded, financed, and conducted his own symphony orchestra in Moscow. He presented monumental festivals in Moscow that became the main artistic events of that city. On his programs some of the most brilliant of the younger Russian composers found a sympathetic hearing, while the music of modern Europeans was being introduced to Russian audiences for the first time. On several occasions, Koussevitzky chartered a steamer and traveled with his orchestra on the Volga, stopping off to give concerts in villages and hamlets which had never before heard a symphony concert. Then, after making history in Russia, he went to Paris, where he organized the Concerts Koussevitzky whose programs were among the most exciting and progressive heard in the French capital. In 1924 Koussevitzky was appointed music director of the Boston Symphony. Under his dynamic, inspiring leadership this renowned orchestra entered on one of its richest epochs, while the American composer had come upon something of a patron saint. Since 1936, Koussevitzky had been directing the Boston Symphony in summer festival performances that attracted to Tanglewood music lovers from all parts of the country.

In the summer of 1940 Koussevitzky added something new to Tanglewood, something which represented for him the fulfillment of a life's dream. This was the Berkshire Music Center, a school where gifted musical students could receive summer training in the performing and creative phases of music; where they could mingle and exchange ideas and experiences with trained musicians and established composers both in the classroom and less formally on the festival grounds. A six-week course in conducting, instrumental performance, composition, and voice was announced for the summer of 1940. Three hundred gifted young men and women came to Tanglewood, many already graduates of leading conservatories, a few even about to fill important music posts.

Under Koussevitzky's over-all direction, the Music Center became at once a unique school of music. Students remained on the grounds of Tanglewood all day, practicing on their instruments in special rooms assigned for that purpose; or else they worked quietly on their lessons while sprawling on the grass. The teachers could usually be found on the grounds at the service of any pupil momentarily stumped by some technical or esthetic problem. A student in composition might be sitting under a tree working on an original piece of music. Aaron Copland, passing by, would glance over his shoulder and possibly then and there make some practical suggestions. Or an instrumentalist might be practicing when a first-desk man of the Boston Symphony would stop off and offer pertinent criticism. Instrumentalists joined chamber music groups and the student orchestra; singers were trained to perform in operas, scenes of operas, oratorios, and other choral music; composers had their works performed; student conductors were given opportunities to practice on and give concerts with the student orchestra.

The conducting class, personally supervised by Koussevitzky, was of course closest to his heart. Some forty students—among them several who already had posts with established orchestras—received both theoretical and practical guidance. Classroom lectures formed one part of this curriculum. Each student was also expected to rehearse the student orchestra several times a semester. He was given a week's notice in which to prepare some given work, and then to rehearse it as if for an actual performance. These young conductors were by no means pampered by assignments consisting of thrice-familiar symphonies, suites, or overtures. They were often assigned highly difficult, sometimes even esoteric, modern compositions. As these young conductors worked on this music with the orchestra, Koussevitzky stood at their elbows with valuable advice on baton technique, platform behavior, technical and esthetic problems posed by the composition being rehearsed, and the most efficient way of instructing the members of the orchestra in solving these problems. All pupil conductors were expected to attend Koussevitzky's own rehearsals with the Boston Symphony, and the concerts as well. They were also encouraged to be present at as many of the lectures, discussions, and student performances taking place on the Tanglewood grounds as possible.

When the opening of this music school was first announced, Koussevitzky also publicized the fact that he was ready to take on five students on a scholarship basis and help prepare them for a professional career. Fritz Reiner's enthusiastic recommendation of Bernstein brought him to Tanglewood as one of the trainees.

That summer of 1940 was probably one of the happiest periods in Bernstein's life up to that time. To move in a musical setting; to work at, talk about, participate in music all his waking hours; to be continually in the presence of, and exchange vital ideas with, inspiring people like Koussevitzky, Copland, and Paul Hindemith (the last, also a member of the faculty, one of the greatest composers of the 20th century)—all this was an experience for Lenny to relish with the delight of a gourmet savoring the taste of Napoleon brandy on the tip of his tongue.

Perhaps the most significant result of that wonderful summer in Tanglewood for Bernstein was the bond that developed early and stayed on permanently between himself and Koussevitzky. Bernstein has never hesitated to acknowledge all that he owes to this great Russian maestro. Koussevitzky's genius as conductor, his imperious and dominating personality, his wholehearted dedication to the highest principles of his art, his passion for modern music all had an inescapable impact on Bernstein. For a long time Bernstein modeled himself after

40

Koussevitzky, even to the point of imitating some of that conductor's more obvious conducting mannerisms. Lenny could hardly have found a worthier model.

At that, the reactions and attitudes of Koussevitzky toward Lenny were unusual for him. He was not the man to give of himself and his love unsparingly; he preferred to surround himself with an impenetrable wall of reserve. Yet "Lenyushka" (as Koussevitzky always called him) became for the older man something of an adopted son—to pamper and spoil and love and boast about.

As a man, as well as a conductor, Koussevitzky was an autocrat who demanded uncompromising allegiance. Intolerant of disagreement or criticism of any kind, he was easy to enrage and difficult to placate. Bernstein was one of the few (if not the only one) who could express a sharp difference of opinion with Koussevitzky and receive, in place of a cyclonic outburst of anger, only a gentle, understanding smile. Once while discussing Bernstein's future as a conductor, Koussevitzky urged him to change his name. Who ever heard of a "Leonard Bernstein" conducting a great orchestra like the Boston Symphony, Koussevitzky asked. Expediency would certainly dictate that Bernstein assume a euphonious, perhaps a Europeanized, name that would set well with symphony audiences. Bernstein told Koussevitzky firmly that if he were to achieve a successful career as a conductor it must come to him under the name with which he was born; he refused to travel to fame under a false identity. It is doubtful if ever before or since anyone vetoed one of Koussevitzky's practical suggestions so decisively without losing the master's favor.

Koussevitzky was, of course, impressed by Lenny's talent, demonstrations of which were without parallel at the Berkshire Music Center that summer. But what perhaps attracted Koussevitzky to Bernstein even more strongly was the young man's expansive and penetrating intelligence in so many areas outside of music. Koussevitzky loved to engage him in all kinds of discussions. He enjoyed Lenny's supreme self-confidence, his excitement over each of his enthusiasms, his continual challenges to authority and tradition. Lenny's fresh wit was for him a perpetual source of amusement.

When Bernstein returned to the Berkshire Music Center for a second semester in the summer of 1941 (after receiving his diploma that June from Curtis Institute), he was once again a member of Koussevitzky's class in conducting. But this time he was recognized as Koussevitzky's protégé. It was rumored that Koussevitzky was seriously thinking of grooming the young man as his successor with the Boston Symphony Orchestra. In any event, Koussevitzky began giving Bernstein increasingly ambitious assignments at Tanglewood. "Ah, Lenyushka," he said one time, "it is time for you to conduct *choeur!*" (By *"choeur"* Koussevitzky meant a major work for chorus and orchestra.) The choice finally fell on a huge, ambitious modern work in a jazz idiom: Constant Lambert's *Rio Grande,* for chorus, orchestra, and solo piano, based on a poem by Sacheverell Sitwell.

Bernstein's last rehearsal of *Rio Grande* took place on the afternoon immediately preceding the actual evening concert. One of those attending that rehearsal was the famous Broadway actress, Tallulah Bankhead, who became so enraptured with Bernstein's performance that when he finished she insisted he come to her nearby summer cottage for dinner. She even refused to wait for him to change his informal rehearsal outfit, which had consisted of dungarees and a basque shirt.

Dinner with Tallulah made Bernstein lose all sense of time. When he looked at his watch he saw to his horror that it was almost eight o'clock. The evening's concert was to begin in a quarter of an hour. Fortunately, his contribution to the program —his performance of *Rio Grande*—did not come until the second half of the program. Even so, there was no time to lose. He was rushed by Tallulah's limousine to his room for a quick change of clothes, and from there he was hurriedly brought to the concert hall. He arrived only a few minutes before he had to mount the conductor's platform.

CHAPTER 7

"This was my Valley Forge"

By the fall of 1941 Bernstein had completed all his formal music study. This was hardly a source of exhilaration. "In a way I was worse off than before. I was a trained conductor. But who hired kid conductors? And if I could not earn a living conducting, then how? I was twenty-three. And I had nowhere to go."

After the Berkshire Music Center closed for the season in August, Koussevitzky urged Bernstein to return to Boston, hoping to find some opportunities for Lenny to prove himself to the public. Koussevitzky was thinking of having Bernstein play the world première of a new piano concerto by Carlos Chávez (Mexico's foremost contemporary composer) on a program for which Chávez had been invited that season to appear as guest conductor of the Boston Symphony. Koussevitzky also planned to have Bernstein conduct one or two concerts of the Boston Symphony.

But in Boston Bernstein confronted only disappointment and frustration. At that time the Boston Symphony was involved in a bitter war with the American Federation of Musicians, the Boston Symphony then being one of the few important American orchestras not yet unionized. James Caesar Petrillo, president of the Federation, had decided the time had come to compel the orchestra to enter the Union fold. No member of the

Musicians Union was henceforth to be permitted to appear with the Boston Symphony in any capacity whatsoever. Since both Chávez and Bernstein were union members their projected engagements with that orchestra had to be canceled. (The irony of this situation did not escape Bernstein. In New York, Bernstein had been unable to get a job because at that time he had not yet become a member of the Musicians Union, while now in Boston he could not get work because he was a member!)

Once again Bernstein's father put severe pressure on Lenny to enter the family business, and once again Lenny's resistance was iron. In an effort to earn some desperately needed money, Bernstein opened a small piano studio on Huntington Avenue in Boston. "I did the usual things. I sent out announcements, and waited for results. Nobody came. *Nobody!*" The main reason for this was that Bernstein had opened his studio on December 5, 1941. Two days later the Japanese bombed Pearl Harbor. America was suddenly at war. Its young people—and their parents—had other thoughts to occupy them than piano lessons.

Soon after Pearl Harbor, Bernstein tried to enlist in the Army. He was summarily turned down because of his congenital asthma, a disappointment he felt so keenly that on returning home he fell onto the living-room couch and burst into tears. Since there was simply no other place for him to go, he lingered on in Boston. He played the piano at some benefit concerts, organized a few musical events at the Institute of Modern Art, including a performance of Copland's little school opera, *The Second Hurricane*. What he earned was not enough to keep him even in pocket money.

He kept busy by practicing the piano industriously and doing some creative work. Since his personal contacts with Paul Hindemith at the Berkshire Music Center had aroused his interest in that composer's music and individual style, Bernstein now tried writing a sonata for clarinet and piano in Hindemith's neoclassical idiom. That sonata later became Bernstein's first published composition. Meanwhile it was also the first of his works to receive a public performance. This took place at the Institute of Modern Art in Boston on April 21, 1942, with David Glazer playing the clarinet part, and Bernstein at the piano.

The winter of 1941 and the spring of 1942 found Bernstein often at Koussevitzky's home in Brookline, Massachusetts—sometimes for lunch or tea, sometimes for an evening with other Koussevitzky friends. The Russian conductor never seemed to lose his delight in being in Lenny's company and in listening to his effervescent and often highly opinionated comments on whatever subject was up for discussion. Vernon Duke, in his autobiography *Passport to Paris,* recalls one such lunch in Brookline. Speaking of Bernstein he wrote: "He had singular and uncompromising views and was fond of airing them in ringing tones, punctuating his statements with a triumphant smile; [Koussevitzky] thrived on that kind of talk from young people and was, in spite of his reputation for a colossal ego, a very good listener. 'Noo, noo, go on. . . .' He'd nudge Bernstein with a wink at me, and Lenny would plunge into boutade after boutade . . . obviously [regarding] his paradoxes as unshakable axioms."

The summer of 1942 proved a welcome respite from his frustrations, for it brought Bernstein back to the congenial setting and the busy musical life of Tanglewood and the Berkshire Music Center. He was a student there no longer, but Koussevitzky's assistant both as a conductor of the Boston Symphony and as a teacher of conducting. That summer went all too quickly. Once again Bernstein's anxiety over his future seized him and made his blood within him freeze. This time he sidestepped Boston to try his luck once more in New York. He knew that if New York could not offer him an opening in music, then he would finally be compelled to go into business after all.

He brought with him to New York several effusive letters of recommendation. One, from Koussevitzky, described him as "a conductor of outstanding talent in whose brilliant future I have great faith." A second, from Reiner, called him a "young musician of extraordinary talents." After renting a furnished room for $8.oo a week, he set forth in search of work—any kind of work so long as it involved music and brought him a fee. He gave lessons in piano or voice for $1.oo an hour. (The sister of the silent motion-picture star, Ramon Novarro, hired him for some vocal coaching for $2.oo an hour.) Two dollars an hour was the price he was paid by ballet dancers for playing the piano at rehearsals. As part of his contribution to the war effort he visited Fort Dix and gave three concerts of boogie-woogie music for the soldiers, without remuneration, of course. He was kept busy—but he could hardly make a living. More than one meal had to be skipped because he did not have the price. Frequently he fell far in arrears in paying his rent. On one occasion he had to send his father a frantic wire asking for $25.oo because, having failed to pay his rent for four weeks, he was about to be dispossessed.

During the winter of 1942 his morale sank to its lowest level; he had arrived at the nadir of his depression. "Bad though the year before had been in Boston—and it had been awful!—I used to walk up and down Broadway and look upon it as heaven. God, how I was miserable in New York!" Again and again he would refer to this period as "my Valley Forge." The hack jobs as teacher and accompanist, the inability to get a hearing as a conductor or a composer, his never-ending tussle with finances—all this scraped and grated on his nerve centers until at moments he felt he would be able to stand this mental torture no longer. There were so many things he wanted to tell people through the medium of music, but nobody cared to listen. In those grim days he finally became convinced that there was no future for him as a musician. Perhaps for the first time he was ready to concede that his father had been right when he said that, in pursuing the mirage of success in music, Lenny would destroy himself both as a human being and as a musician.

He was pondering this unhappy situation, and inwardly bemoaning his fate, one day while walking along Broadway. Suddenly he came upon a casual acquaintance, Irving Caesar. Caesar was a successful song lyricist who had written the words for many outstanding popular songs including George Gershwin's "Swanee" and Vincent Youmans' "Tea for Two." Schoolchildren everywhere are perhaps even more familiar with his name through his "Safety Songs." In any event, earlier that year, Caesar had come to Boston for the out-of-town tryouts of a musical comedy which starred Adolph Green and Betty Comden and for which he had written the lyrics. After the Boston première of this show, Green brought Bernstein to a party at the Ritz-Carlton Hotel, where Lenny was introduced to Caesar. As was habitual, Bernstein soon went over to the piano. Irving Caesar listened to him spellbound and at the time described Bernstein as "a genius."

Apparently, Irving Caesar had forgotten neither Bernstein nor his informal performance at the Ritz-Carlton. As they crossed directions on Broadway, Caesar recognized him at once. When Bernstein told Caesar of his inability to get a job, the latter said he would help. And he did. A few days later, Caesar introduced Bernstein to Herman Starr, a power in the music-publishing business as the head of the Music Publishers Holding Corporation, a combine of several famous popular-music publishing establishments. Starr hired Bernstein, at a salary of $25.00 a week, to work for Harms-Remick, a branch of the corporation. (Later on Starr also became Bernstein's publisher and business adviser.) Bernstein's job was to arrange popular songs for piano, two and four hands; to make band transcriptions; to put down on paper improvisations by such jazz men as Earl Hines and Coleman Hawkins. Some of his work was published, all of it under the pen name of "Lenny Amber" ("amber being the English translation of the German word, "Bern," the first syllable of Bernstein's surname).

The security of a regular income brought Bernstein temporary elation. Now that he knew where his next meal and his next week's rent would come from, he was able to give up his sordid furnished room for a more comfortable, cheerful, and convenient studio apartment in the Carnegie Hall building.

He threw himself into extracurricular musical activities with a renewed outburst of energy. They might pay him little or nothing whatsoever, but they did provide him with the immense personal satisfaction of expressing himself through serious music and making contact with an audience. Several times he appeared as pianist over WNYC (the New York City municipal radio station), once with David Oppenheim, clarinetist, in a performance of his clarinet sonata. On February 17, 1943 he appeared in Town Hall, New York, at a forum-concert presided over by Virgil Thomson devoted to the music of Aaron Copland, where he played Copland's Piano Sonata. Bernstein was not originally selected to give the performance. But a day or so before concert time, the scheduled pianist fell ill, and Bernstein was hastily recruited as a substitute. He learned the immense and technically exacting work in a matter of hours, and gave a brilliant account of both himself and Copland's music; he even contributed some charming verbal comments about Aaron Copland and the sonata.

In March, Bernstein appeared at the Museum of Modern Art in a special program devoted to Camargo Guarnieri, a distinguished South American composer. In the same month he appeared at a concert of music by Young Americans, sponsored by the League of Composers at the New York Public Library, where once again he participated in a presentation of his clarinet sonata. In May he filled the dual role of pianist-commentator at a benefit concert in Town Hall. And so it went.

Nor was composition neglected. During 1943 he wrote and had published by Witmark a song cycle, *I Hate Music: Five Kid Songs*. (Witmark had previously also published his clarinet sonata.) But his most ambitious composition of all that year was a major work—and his first—for symphony orchestra. While completed in 1942 it had been begun a few years earlier. In the summer of 1939 he projected and sketched a composition for soprano and orchestra called *Lamentation,* on a text from the Book of Lamentations in the Bible. The music remained just random sketches. Early in 1942 Bernstein learned that the New England Conservatory in Boston was sponsoring a contest among American composers for a symphonic work. After deciding to enter the contest he mulled over various ideas, finally planning the writing of a symphony inspired by the Biblical prophet, Jeremiah. Once this idea was crystallized in his mind he realized that the *Lamentation* he had started in 1939 and never finished could fit in nicely as the last movement of his symphony.

The deadline for the submission of entries to the contest was December 31, 1942. Bernstein had to work at top speed. Most of the *Jeremiah Symphony* was written in white-heat intensity, and with a momentum that often kept Bernstein working through half the night. The orchestration was completed during ten days of feverish work. All the while Bernstein kept himself awake at night by drinking numerous cups of coffee and stimulating his nervous system with benzedrine pills. When his manuscript had to be prepared, friends came to his help. They drew the bar lines and assisted in inking in the notes. Shirley Bernstein wrote in the time signatures. Bernstein personally delivered his manuscript to the New England Conservatory in Boston at the zero hour— just before midnight on December 31. The next day he took the train back to New York and went straight to bed to recover from his physical and mental exhaustion.

There had been exhilaration in writing his first symphony, just as there had been exhilaration in getting his first job and making his first New York appearances as a pianist and a composer. But this happy state was short-lived. By late spring of 1943 he was once again in the doldrums. His symphony did not win the prize. Worse still, Koussevitzky, who had seen the manuscript, had told him bluntly he did not like it. Now the despondency of 1942 deepened into outright despair, from which there would be no escape that summer. Both the Berkshire Symphony Festival and the Berkshire Music Center had that year suspended operations for the duration of the war.

Nonetheless, Bernstein did go back to Lenox, Massachusetts, that August. Koussevitzky was giving there a series of three lecture-recitals for the benefit of the Red Cross, and he had invited Bernstein to provide the musical illustrations at the piano. En route to Lenox, Bernstein dropped off at Boston to make one more attempt to get into the Army. Once again he was turned down. This rejection put him in an ugly mood when he arrived in Lenox on Saturday morning. An agonizing cold did not help matters either. The following day was August 25—his twenty-fifth birthday. A happy birthday, indeed! Despite all his frantic efforts of the past year he had failed to penetrate the fringe of New York's concert life, and he was now farther than ever from a successful career.

On arriving in Lenox, Bernstein received a message from Koussevitzky that Artur Rodzinski, resting at his farm in nearby Stockbridge, wanted to see him the following morning. Rodzinski was one of America's outstanding conductors who had just been appointed as the new music director of the New York Philharmonic.

When Bernstein came to Stockbridge to meet Rodzinski the next morning, they sat in the fields "on a kind of haystack." For a while they talked aimlessly. Rodzinski revealed he had heard Bernstein conduct the student orchestra at Tanglewood and had been impressed. They continued on with a rambling conversation when Rodzinski suddenly turned to Bernstein and asked:

51

"How would you like to be assistant conductor of the New York Philharmonic next season?"

It had come as simply as all that: the turning point in Bernstein's life; the beginning of his professional career in music; the ending of all his doubts, fears, frustrations, and despair! Rodzinski had not even questioned him about his ability to take on the assistant conductor's job. Bernstein had not played the piano for him nor gone through any scores. And yet one of the most desirable jobs in the country had fallen into his lap like a ripe plum from a top-heavy tree! His salary of $100 a week spelled financial security for Bernstein at long last. The post further provided a cherished opportunity to work with one of the world's greatest orchestras in making music! Surely this was the gift of gifts for his twenty-fifth birthday!

Since good fortune rarely comes unattended, Bernstein was given a second birthday gift that same evening. At the lecture-concert in Lenox, Koussevitzky gave him the opportunity to give the first public presentation of his song cycle, *I Hate Music,* with Jennie Tourel as soloist.

A few days later a brief announcement was published in *The New York Times* to the effect that Leonard Bernstein, who never before had conducted a professional symphony orchestra in public, was appointed Artur Rodzinski's assistant with the New York Philharmonic. The notice went on to say that Bernstein was the youngest man ever to receive this appointment with this historic orchestra.

Bernstein tore the clipping out of the newspaper and sent it to Helen Coates in Boston. At the top of the clipping he scrawled in red ink: "Here we go!"

But how far he was going—and how quickly—not even he, in his wildest imagination or in his most uninhibited dreams, could have dared to anticipate.

CHAPTER 8

"Here we go!"

Leonard Bernstein became assistant conductor of the New York Philharmonic Orchestra in the fall of 1943. He had, at last, good cause for contentment. For the first time he was making a respectable living from music without the necessity of resorting to hack work. His main duty at the Philharmonic was to read the new scores that came into the office, sifting out those he thought worthy of performance. Thus he found himself in the mainstream of contemporary music, and he enjoyed to the full the stimulation of studying and passing on the music of composers both world-famous and unknown. Beyond all this, he now had a magnificent orchestra to work with and experiment on—for he was required to be present at all rehearsals and sometimes take over and help Rodzinski in preparing a composition. The only thing still lacking to make his musical life complete was an audience to communicate with —since all his work ended at rehearsals—something which his personality and temperament demanded as relentlessly as his body needed food and rest. But now he was fully convinced that he would get that audience sooner or later. It came much sooner than even he had dared to hope.

On the evening of Saturday, November 13, Bernstein accompanied Jennie Tourel in the concert première of his song cycle, *I Hate Music,* at Town Hall, New York. His parents had come from Boston for this concert, the Philharmonic appointment having finally convinced them that Lenny was a musician to reckon with. For Bernstein their presence contributed additional zest to the excitement of presenting his composition to a sophisticated New York audience.

Later that night Bernstein attended a party at Jennie Tourel's apartment. There he was the center of interest, surrounded and continually congratulated for his music by admiring friends and acquaintances. He was snatched from them by the telephone. Bruno Zirato, manager of the Philharmonic, had called to say that Bruno Walter, then appearing as the guest conductor of the orchestra, was sick in bed and would be unable to appear at his concert the following afternoon. Efforts were now being made, Zirato said, to reach Artur Rodzinski at his Stockbridge farm. If Rodzinski were unable to come into the city the next morning to take over the performance, then Bernstein would have to substitute.

At the moment when he moodily restored the telephone receiver to its carriage, the possibility that he might be called on to conduct the New York Philharmonic the next day seemed highly remote. There was no reason in the world why Rodzinski could not be contacted; no reason why there was not enough time for Rodzinski to make the four-hour motor trip into New York the next morning well in time for him to conduct the afternoon concert. Nevertheless, Bernstein cautiously decided to leave Tourel's party at once, go back to his studio, and glance through the scores of the music being performed the next day—"just in case," as he said. Scheduled on that program was a world première: *Theme and Variations* by a young Hungarian-born American now working in Hollywood, Miklós Rózsa. In addition, there were Schumann's *Manfred Overture,* Richard Strauss' *Don Quixote,* and Wagner's Prelude to *Die Meistersinger.*

"I stayed up until about 4:30 a.m., alternately dozing, sipping coffee, and studying the scores. I fell into a sound sleep about 5:30 a.m. and awakened at 9 a.m. An hour later Mr. Zirato telephoned and said, 'You're going to conduct.' My first reaction was one of shock. I then became very excited over my unexpected debut and, I may add, not a little frightened. Knowing it would be impossible to assemble the orchestra for a rehearsal on a Sunday, I went over to Mr. Walter's home and went over the scores with him. I found Mr. Walter sitting up but wrapped in blankets and he obligingly showed me just how he did it."

After this brief session with Bruno Walter, Bernstein returned to his studio for another few hours of study. At 11 a.m. he called his father, who was staying at the Barbizon Hotel and was planning to return to Boston that afternoon. "You're going to see me conduct the Philharmonic," Lenny told him excitedly. Finally, at 1:30 p.m. he pushed aside the music and began to dress. He put on a conservative gray sack suit, the best outfit he had available. (As yet he did not own either a dinner jacket or a cutaway.) He was in a state of physical exhaustion for lack of sufficient sleep. He was tense with fear, nervousness, and excitement. His emotions were keyed to a high pitch. And he was suffering from a stuffed nose.

In an effort to quiet his nerves, he stopped off at the drugstore near Carnegie Hall for a cup of coffee. Then he made his way through the 56th Street entrance to Carnegie Hall to the artist's room, there to await the summons to the stage which came promptly at three o'clock. With a slight nod of recognition to the applause that greeted him, he moved energetically across the stage and leaped briskly to the conductor's dais.

When Bruno Zirato stepped on the stage to announce that Bruno Walter was ill and that "you are going to witness the debut of a full-fledged conductor born, educated, and trained in this country," many in the audience that day knew little about Bernstein. They could, then, hardly have expected more than a perfunctory performance. Even some of those in the hall who knew him well and were fully aware of his immense talent remained skeptical of his results that afternoon. After all, Bernstein was about to meet his first serious test as the conductor of a major symphony orchestra under the most severe conditions possible —probably more severe than those ever before encountered by any other young conductor making a debut. Bernstein was directing a program he had not rehearsed. He was conducting some music with which he had first become acquainted only a few hours earlier. And he lacked the experience necessary to give him the assurance and skill he would need to meet such a challenge.

The first loud chords of the *Manfred Overture* sounded brilliant and precise. Bernstein says that the moment those first notes rang out he lost all feeling of nervousness and doubt, all consciousness of the awesome fact that at long last he was on the stage of Carnegie Hall conducting the New York Philharmonic Orchestra before an audience, that at the other end of the microphone dangling over his head were several million more music lovers across the length and breadth of the United States. All that mattered to him now was the music itself—as he was shaping and carving it with his beautifully articulated, batonless hands.

Two hours after that the majestic closing chords of Wagner's Prelude to *Die Meistersinger* brought the concert to a triumphant conclusion. A thunderous ovation followed, growing in strength all the time like some gathering storm. The young, exhausted conductor—drenched to his skin with perspiration— bowed first to the cheering audience, and then to his parents seated in the auditorium. His strong, handsome, expressive face was radiant. At that moment he knew that all the defeats of the past had been resolved into a magnificent victory; all the doubts that had preceded this day, and whose overpowering weight had been so crushing, had now been replaced by self-confidence and an unshakable faith in the future.

56

That concert was transmitted over the network of the Columbia Broadcasting System. Koussevitzky was in that radio audience. He was one of the first to send in his congratulations. He wired simply: "Listening Now. Wonderful." Artur Rodzinski appeared in Carnegie Hall during intermission. He heard only the second half of the concert, after which his verdict was: "Bernstein is a prodigious talent."

Such were the initial stirrings of what soon became a veritable deluge of acclaim. Newspapermen, even representatives of the foreign press, rushed backstage to talk to Bernstein before relaying to their papers their stories of a phenomenal event. Eight crews of photographers—no one seemed to know why they were there and where they had suddenly come from— were taking over a hundred pictures of the young conductor. *The New York Times* and the New York *Herald Tribune* were two of several newspapers to carry the story on their first page as a news event of first importance. *The New York Times* also devoted an editorial to the debut; and its critic, Olin Downes, discussed the performance in a full-column review.

What Downes said that day reflected the reaction of his colleagues. Bernstein "shows that he is one of the very few conductors of the rising generation who are indubitably to be reckoned with. . . . It was clear at once that . . . he was conducting the orchestra in his own right and not the orchestra conducting him; that he had everyone of the scores both in his hands and his head; and though he logically and inevitably conformed in broad outline, he was not following slavishly in the footsteps of his distinguished senior. Mr. Bernstein thought for himself and obtained his wishes. . . . The program was exacting . . . [but] was met with a fine comprehension, with emotional as well as intellectual flexibility, and the perception of line, proportion, climax which drove the music home. And there was the interpretative artist's conviction which establishes its truth."

The New York *Daily News* was more colloquial in its report—reaching out for an analogue in baseball in much the same way Bernstein himself would someday be doing while making a musical commentary. Said *The News:* "Like a shoestring catch in the centerfield—make it and you're a hero. Muff it and you're a dope. Bernstein made it."

"Why Is a Conductor Necessary?"

Leonard Bernstein was now a famous conductor. This, then, may be the convenient moment in his story to pause momentarily and digress long enough to consider the art of conducting. What are the qualities that make a conductor "great"?

In his telecast on December 4, 1955, in which he discussed and analyzed this very question, Bernstein opened his program by directing the first pages of Brahms' Symphony No. 1. Suddenly he stopped conducting and walked away from the podium. But the orchestra continued to play as if nothing had happened—and playing both accurately and well. "You see," remarked Bernstein, "they don't need me. They do perfectly well by themselves." Then he went on to ask: "Why is a conductor necessary?"

The men of a great symphony orchestra are, to be sure, all highly trained musicians fully capable of reading music and counting time. And, with proper preparation, they would still be able to play correctly if there were no conductor standing in front of them giving them directions. In fact, some decades ago, several attempts were made to dispense with conductors, with "conductorless orchestras" in the Soviet Union and later on in New York. These concerts were all technically efficient. The notes were all there, in correct time and proper balance. But if the music had a recognizable body, what it lacked was a soul. However meticulously rehearsed these concerts had been, the music in perfomance had lost that spark of vitality, that subtlety of expression and nuance, and that power of fresh communication with which even a thrice-familiar piece of music becomes vibrant and alive and exciting when re-created by a gifted interpreter. The "conductorless orchestra" passed out of existence; it is extremely doubtful if it will ever again return.

A conductor, then, *is* necessary. What, then, is his function? And what are the means by which he tries to achieve it?

Obviously he is the man who must keep the orchestra together by gestures that enunciate the correct tempo and rhythm. For ages—up to the middle of the 19th century—the conductor was primarily a time-beater, or *"Taktschlaeger"* as the Germans called him. Many were the ways in which, through the years, time was beaten. "One man conducts with the foot," wrote Johann Baehr in 1719, "another with the head, a third with the hand, some with both hands, some again take a roll of paper, others with a stick." In the Sistine Chapel in the 16th century conductors beat time with a roll of paper called the "sol-fa." In the 17th, Jean-Baptiste Lully beat time at the Paris Opéra by pounding his walking stick on the floor. One century later, time was beaten by the musician playing the harpsichord, organ, or even the first violin—with brisk gestures of the head when he was playing his instrument, with motions of the hand when he had no music to play.

The baton first came into vogue in 1820. In this development the pioneer was Louis Spohr, come to London as guest conductor of the Royal Philharmonic Orchestra. Instead of directing his performance from the concertmaster's seat as was habitual in England, Spohr stood in front of his men and, to their amazement, beat out for them the patterns of time and rhythm by waving a little stick in the air. "Quite alarmed at such a novel proceeding," recalled Spohr in his autobiography, "the directors protested against it, but when I besought them to grant me at least one trial they became pacified. . . . I . . . could not only give the tempi in a very decisive manner, but indicated also to the wind instruments and horns all the entries, which ensured to them a confidence such as hitherto they had not known. . . . Incited thereby to more than attention, and conducted with certainty by the *visible* manner of giving the time, they played with a spirit and correctness such as, until then, they had never before been heard to play. Surprised and inspired by the result, the orchestra, immediately after the first part of the symphony, expressed aloud its unified assent to the new mode of conducting, and thereby overruled all further opposition on the part of the directors. . . . The triumph of the baton as a time-giver was decisive."

That little stick, and the patterns fashioned in midair by Spohr, represent a milestone in the history of conducting and orchestral performance. The conductor, no longer required to play an instrument in or with the orchestra, could direct all his attention both on the music he was interpreting and on the men who were performing it. Thus the conductor began rapidly to acquire a new status, which he was not slow to exploit. Before long there now appeared on the scene conductors like Felix Mendelssohn in Leipzig, Hector Berlioz in France, and Franz Liszt in Weimar, who supplemented the function of time-beating with the imposition on the men of the orchestra their own concepts of the music they were performing. These conductors helped develop and perfect baton technique to the point where they could telegraph some of these demands to their musicians while beating time. They initiated exacting rehearsals in which the orchestra could be trained in the technical demands of the music and problems of style could be worked

61

out. With Richard Wagner, the personal stamp of the conductor—his individual interpretation of any given piece of music—was even more strongly than heretofore impressed on performances. The conductor was a time-beater no more. He was now an interpreter, and re-creator, in the finest sense of the term.

Today the conductor is the catalytic agent between the printed page of music and the men who play it. He and he alone must decide on all the subtleties of tempo, rhythm, accent, dynamics, retards and accelerations, orchestral balance, and over-all style. To put it as simply as possible: He must know how an orchestral work should sound both down to its very essentials and up to its grand design; after that he must know how to bring that sound to life. A pianist or a violinist, for example, do the very same things on their instruments. But the conductor is unique in that he must do this through *other* musicians and to coalesce them into a single entity.

To do his job properly, a conductor must first be endowed with certain anatomical equipment. He must have an ear sensitive to musical tones, textures, and colors—even more so, in fact, than other musical interpreters, since he must have the capacity to pierce through the most complex labyrinth of orchestral sound and recognize the slightest deviation from the acceptable. A conductor who cannot hear even in loudest passages a wrong note, an improper accent, an inexact rhythm, or a poor adjustment of orchestral balance can hardly hope to achieve a desirable performance.

Then a conductor must have a brain. His knowledge of music must embrace some working acquaintance with many, if not most, of the instruments of the orchestra so that at all times he knows what each instrument is capable of doing, and how. Through a knowledge of music history and backgrounds, the conductor must be able to understand and appreciate different styles of different composers: the serene and ordered classicism of a Haydn or a Mozart on the one hand, or the uninhibited emotional outpourings of a Mahler or a Bruckner on the other; the religious exaltation of a Bach on the one hand and the sensuality of a Wagner on the other; the dramatic thought of a Beethoven or a Brahms on the one hand and the ordered mental processes of modernists like Hindemith and Stravinsky on the other. Finally, the conductor must know the score of each work he is conducting down to the smallest detail. He must be able to read that score with facility and have the capacity to translate in his inner ear the printed page into musical sound and, conversely, musical sound into the printed page. Someone once put it very well when he said that a conductor must be able "to hear with his eyes and read with his ears." All this does not mean that a conductor must necessarily direct performances from memory. But it does mean that both at rehearsals and concerts he must know the music so thoroughly that he need not continually consult the score in front of him to know what is coming next. Thus he is in the position of focusing his undivided concentration on both the music and the orchestra.

A conductor must also have heart. His emotional response to each composition he plays must be highly sensitized. He must feel the music in every pore and fiber of his being, believe in it, love it. Only then can he hope to transfer to the orchestra men the emotional impact a given work has made on him.

Ear, brain, and heart, then, are important. But they alone—however highly developed—cannot create a great conductor. In addition to all these things, a conductor must be a dynamic, exciting, inspiring personality. He must be able to electrify his orchestra. Bernstein himself has put it this way: "He must exalt them, lift them, start their adrenal pouring." A conductor may have the most exact technical knowledge and the most exalted artistic concept of a composition but if he cannot excite and inspire his men the result can hardly be more than a perfunctory performance. If any proof is needed for this contention, it will be found in the fact that so many composers are only second-rate performers of their own music. Surely few know the scores better than the composers themselves; surely few are as intimately acquainted with its most subtle or elusive emotional and intellectual content as the composers themselves; surely nobody knows better than the composer how a piece of music *should* sound. Besides, most composers are sound technicians as conductors, having had intensive training and experience in this direction. Yet when they perform their own works the result usually is not half so exciting or compelling as when a great conductor interprets them.

Beyond his personal magnetism, a conductor—like every other genius—must have the capacity to take infinite pains. He must never be content with the second best, must remain ever relentless in the hunt for perfection. He must be able to bring the same freshness, youth, joy, and love to a musical composition performing it a hundredth time as he did when he first discovered it.

In order to penetrate to the very heart of a masterwork—to comprehend its over-all emotional and intellectual design—a conductor must have behind him a lifetime of thought, feeling, and experience. In making music he must continually draw deeply from the well of a cultural background. This is what Bruno Walter meant when he said that "to know Beethoven, you must also know *Hamlet* and Goethe." A provincial mind can never recreate the noble concepts of a Bach, a Beethoven, or a Brahms without revealing its own limitations and narrowness. The greatest conductors of the world have all been men of immense wisdom, intellectual maturity, cosmic viewpoints. As Dimitri Mitropoulos once said: "The conductor in himself is nothing. It is the infinite amount of culture back of him that is the conductor."

64

A conductor's work is done mainly at rehearsals. It is then that he clarifies for his orchestra men all the technical problems in a work; elucidates for them its artistic design; penetrates for them to its very essence in search of inner meanings. In the last analysis, what a conductor is trying to do with all the resources, knowledge, and technique at his command is to bring to life what a composer has put down on paper; and to uncover the subtleties and nuances of expression and meaning which a composer intended in his music but which the printed page cannot always convey with exactitude. To articulate what is in the music is the supreme achievement of the great musical interpreter. It is only the second-rater who tries to personalize and dramatize his performances with excessive alterations of tempo, rhythm, dynamics; with a prolix use of rubatos; with exaggerations of accelerations and crescendos, rallentandos and diminuendos.

At the performance itself, the conductor must call on silent gestures alone in communicating with his musicians. Though most of the work in the preparation of a composition is over, at the concert the conductor must still engage himself in the business of re-creation and interpretation. Efficient pronunciation of tempo and rhythm, and discreet cues, help to keep the musicians in line. Other gestures must maintain in the orchestra the spirit of excitement or exaltation the conductor had previously engendered at rehearsals. A knowledgeable conductor can, even while a performance is taking place, make his final adjustments in sonority, balances, changes of tempo. But to do this he must be able to hear clearly in his mind two things simultaneously: the music that is being played at that moment and the music that will be played in the next few bars.

No one recognizes and can evaluate the true worth of a conductor as the musician who plays under him. The orchestra player knows when a conductor has given him a new insight into a familiar piece of music; when the conductor has lifted him and made him soar to new heights in his performance. When confronted with greatness in the conductor, the orchestra becomes as idolatrous as any ordinary music lover. More than once has an arduous, nerve-wracking rehearsal ended with an orchestra rising spontaneously to cheer its conductor. The heat of the battle is over. What remains unforgettable to the men is the victory of having a musical composition rise from the printed page to the elevation of a palpitant work of art.

PART TWO

"*Made Glorious Summer by This Sun...*"

CHAPTER 9

"I live in a schizophrenic world"

In less than a year after his momentous debut, Leonard Bernstein was able to establish his reputation solidly not only as a conductor but even as a composer.

Once, while discussing with an interviewer his two main areas of musical activity—conducting and composing—Bernstein described himself as a musician with a split personality. "A performer," he explained, "is a highly public figure, an extrovert, whose whole compulsion is to get out there in front of people and let it out. Now a creative person is quite another fellow. He has a complex inner life, his big relationship being with himself, or his Muse, or his God, or his subconscious. He has to seek out that gray solitude where he's stuck with himself. Most people of the arts belong to one group or the other. I live in a schizophrenic world of both."

Before the year 1943 had ended, Bernstein was given several more opportunities to conduct the Philharmonic, this time in carefully rehearsed performances. On December 2, 3, and 4 he conducted a single number, Ernest Bloch's *Three Jewish Poems;* on December 16 and 17 he was assigned virtually the entire program, except for a single composition then being introduced by its own composer.

Bernstein was also invited to appear with leading orchestras throughout the United States and Canada. On February 18 and 19, 1944 he made his first appearances with the Boston Symphony. Early in March he conducted in Montreal. Between March 29 and April 27 he led four more concerts of the New York Philharmonic. On May 7 he was featured in the dual role of pianist and conductor at a concert of the Boston Pops Orchestra. It was on this occasion that he played and conducted for the first time the Ravel G major Piano Concerto, a work and a performance with which he has since circled the music world. During July he was a guest conductor at Ravinia Park, Chicago, the Lewisohn Stadium in New York, the Montreal Symphony, and the New York Ballet Theater in Los Angeles. In less than a year after his New York Philharmonic debut he had traveled over 50,000 miles and conducted almost one hundred performances. The promises of his spectacular debut were thus glowingly fulfilled as with each appearance he demonstrated an ever increasing command of his conducting technique and powers of interpretation. In Virgil Thomson, music critic of the New York *Herald Tribune*—as in most other music critics everywhere else—Bernstein already inspired early in 1944 full confidence "in . . . his genius as an executant and an interpreter."

His alter ego—the composer—was also beginning to flourish under the beneficent sun of public and critical acclaim.

When Bernstein went to Pittsburgh late in January 1944 for guest performances, he took with him the manuscript of his

Jeremiah Symphony for its world première. (Jennie Tourel was the vocal soloist.) This work—in a romantic, rhapsodic style, and rich in emotional content—was a dramatic contrast to the ultramodern idiom and neoclassic restraint of his preceding clarinet sonata. The three movements were respectively entitled "Prophecy," "Profanation," and "Lamentation"—the last utilizing a verbal text from the Book of Lamentations sung by a mezzo-soprano. Though this symphony was pervaded throughout with intense racial feeling, Bernstein rarely used actual Hebrew melodies. There were two exceptions. The first theme of the second movement a phrase was lifted from a traditional synagogual chant for the Sabbath sung during the reading of the *Haftorah*. And the opening phrase of the vocal part of the finale was derived from a liturgical cadence heard on *Tisha B'Av*, the holiday commemorating the destruction of Jerusalem. "Other resemblances to Hebrew liturgical music are a matter of emotional quality rather than of the notes themselves," Bernstein has explained. "The first movement aims only to parallel in feeling the intensity of the prophet Jeremiah's pleas with his people; and the Scherzo, to give the general sense of destruction and chaos brought up by the pagan corruption within the priesthood and the people. The third movement being a setting of the poetic text is naturally a more literary conception. It is the cry of Jeremiah as he mourns his beloved Jerusalem, ruined, pillaged, and dishonored after his desperate efforts to save it."

Following these initial performances in Pittsburgh, the symphony was heard in many other American cities. Bernstein introduced it to Boston when, on February 18 and 19, he made his first appearances with the Boston Symphony. (It was characteristic of Koussevitzky's broad tolerance to modern music in general and to his "Lenyushka" in particular that though he had not taken to the *Jeremiah Symphony* when he first saw it in manuscript—and thus would not himself conduct it—he was nevertheless eager to have Bernstein conduct it at his Boston debut.) On March 29, 31, and April 1, New York heard the symphony when Bernstein directed guest performances of the New York Philharmonic.

The *Jeremiah Symphony* continued to get numerous performances during the next few years. Wherever it was heard it made a profound impression. Everywhere the critics found this music to be "moving in fervor," "spacious in design," of a "lyrical intensity," and filled "with real exuberance and zest."

The distinguished Boston critic, Warren Story Smith, wrote: "In commenting upon what seemed to him a real significant occasion, this reviewer finds himself in the predicament of the symphony man who is said to have remarked that he didn't dare say how good he thought Mr. Bernstein was for fear of appearing ridiculous. However, he is willing to go all overboard and quote Schumann's famous salutation to Chopin, 'Hats off, gentlemen, a genius!' We do not know whether he will surpass or even equal his first symphonic effort. But no matter. The real point is that one cannot think offhand of any other American composition that has the drive, the poignancy, the dramatic strength, the emotional force of this *Jeremiah*."

Modern Music said: "With unwavering simplicity and directness he has written not so much a literal expression of a Biblical excerpt as he has fashioned an emotional experience of his own. . . . The tense austerity of the first movement, the fresh charm of the . . . theme which opens the Scherzo, and the expressive simplicity of the final movement standout."

Virgil Thomson reported: "Mr. Bernstein orchestrates like a master. The symphony has . . . lyrical intensity; and at the beginning of the middle, or Scherzo, section there is a sort of dance passage that evokes most poignantly the Jewish Near East."

On May 16, 1944, the symphony received the New York Music Critics Circle Award as "the outstanding orchestral work by an American composer" introduced that season—a

70

selection made on the very first ballot. In 1945, RCA Victor released a recording, in a performance by the St. Louis Symphony under Bernstein, Nan Merriman soloist. When the three-day rehearsal of *Jeremiah* ended in St. Louis, the men of the orchestra rose to their feet to cheer the young composer-conductor. "I just stood there on the podium and wept," Bernstein says.

Bernstein's first symphony was soon followed by his first ballet score. On April 18, 1944, Bernstein conducted the world première of *Fancy Free* at the Metropolitan Opera House in New York.

He had been commissioned to write this score by the Ballet Theater (now called the American Ballet Theater). With his commitments as conductor now a serious drain on his time, he was compelled to write much of this music by fits and starts, in many different parts of the country. Some was done on trains, in airports, in hotel rooms between appointments with interviewers and late at night after his concerts. His progress was further complicated by the fact that Jerome Robbins (who was preparing the choreography) was himself pretty much on the move with the touring Ballet Theater; and a second collaborator (Oliver Smith, scenic designer) was at that time in Mexico. The three men had to co-ordinate their separate efforts on *Fancy Free* by means of long-distance telephone, by telegraph, and even by recordings. As soon as Bernstein finished a section of music he recorded it and dispatched the disc to Robbins wherever he happened to be at the time. Robbins then wired Bernstein his comments and possible suggestions for revision. After Bernstein had made these changes, a new recording would be sent Robbins. Other ideas between composer and choreographer had to be discussed over the telephone. Sudden inspirations on the part of one came winging across the country in wires to the other. All the while both Robbins and Bernstein had to maintain continual communication with Smith in Mexico.

Fancy Free is a ballet of young America in 1944. Bernstein goes on to describe the action as follows: "With the sound of a juke box . . . the curtain rises on a street corner with a lamp post, a side street bar, and New York skyscrapers pricked out with a crazy pattern of lights, making a dizzying background. Three sailors explode on the stage; they are on shore leave in the city and on the prowl for girls. The tale of how they meet first one, then a second girl, and how they fight over them, lose them, and in the end take off after still a third, is the story of the ballet."

In writing his music Bernstein revealed still a new string to his creative lyre. The austere and modern approaches of the clarinet sonata, and the romantic and racial style of his symphony, were displaced by the highly spiced melodies, rhythms, and instrumental colors of jazz. Since all his life Bernstein enjoyed playing and improvising on the piano jazz melodies, the blues, and boogie-woogie, writing in these popular styles came to him naturally.

His often brilliant, always deeply musical, and ever sophisticated use of jazz was one reason why *Fancy Free* was such an immediate success. Another was Jerome Robbins' imaginative choreography. This was his bow in a field in which he would soon achieve world-wide eminence. Edwin Denby of the New York *Herald Tribune* described *Fancy Free* as "a perfect American character ballet." John Martin of *The New York Times* said it was "a rare little genre masterpiece." George Amberg, in his book *Ballet,* called it the "first substantial ballet entirely created in the contemporary American idiom, a striking and beautifully convincing example of genuine American style."

Bernstein was originally scheduled to direct only seven performances of *Fancy Free*—the spring season of the Ballet Theater being scheduled to close on May 7. But the overwhelming acclaim to *Fancy Free* and the persistent demand for tickets necessitated the extension of the Ballet Theater season for an additional two weeks. During this period Bernstein was called on to direct twelve more performances. In June, Bernstein recorded his score for Decca, and in July he appeared for two weeks with the Ballet Theater at the Hollywood Bowl in California. *Fancy Free* was given 161 times in its first full season. Since then it has become a staple in the modern American ballet repertory.

When the New York Music Critics Circle met in 1944 to select the *Jeremiah Symphony* for its annual award, it seriously considered bestowing on Bernstein a second prize—for the best new ballet music of the season. After mature deliberation, however, the critics decided against such a move, feeling it unwise on their part to confer two such important honors in the same year to a young and unknown composer.

One other serious Bernstein composition was introduced in 1944: *Seven Anniversaries,* a suite for solo piano, completed one year earlier. These were brief anniversary tributes to seven close to him, including Copland, Shirley Bernstein, Serge Koussevitzky, and William Schuman. All were written in a comparatively modern idiom, the dissonances and unorthodox tonalities, however, severely disciplined by a sound feeling for structure. A critic for *The New York Times* called these pieces "slight" but went on to say that they were written "with charm and grace, and obviously inspired by the personal qualities of the people to whom they are dedicated." Bernstein himself played this work for the first time, at a benefit concert at the Boston Opera House on May 14, 1944. A half year later, on October 13, Gordon Manley gave its official première at Town Hall, New York. In 1948, Bernstein wrote four more anniversary pieces for piano.

Having gathered accolades for his first symphony and his first ballet score, Bernstein was now preparing to enter a new creative arena, one not often accessible to serious musicians: the Broadway musical comedy.

Soon after *Fancy Free* was produced, Adolph Green and Betty Comden discussed with Bernstein the possibility of expanding the lively textual material of the ballet into a musical comedy. From the very beginning of these talks, this idea excited Bernstein. He had always loved musical comedy, had always enjoyed singing and playing the show tunes of the past. The urge to write popular music of his own for the Broadway stage was too irresistible to be denied.

During the summer of 1944, Bernstein went to the hospital for an operation on a deviated septum. His room was always crowded with friends, popping in and out at all hours of the day and evening as if they were coming to a cocktail party. The room was continually ringing with laughter, loud talk, arguments, the playing of the radio at full blast, shouts from gin-rummy games. One harassed nurse remarked wearily that Bernstein might very well be "God's gift to music but I hate to tell you where he gives me a pain."

Despite the crowds, the noise, and the activities swirling all around him—despite the necessary medical preparations for his operation and the discomfort and pain that came with convalescence—Bernstein was able to begin working on his musical comedy in the hospital. As it happened, Adolph Green was required at this very same time to have his tonsils removed. Green and Bernstein took adjoining hospital rooms and arranged for their respective operations to take place on the same day, so that they could take full advantage of all their free time in bed to work on their musical. Betty Comden was the unifying agent for their often excited discussions and plans. She would continually rush from Green's room to Bernstein's and back again to Green's carrying new ideas and fresh pieces of stage business while contributing suggestions of her own.

The writing of the musical comedy went so quickly and

effortlessly once they left the hospital that it was scheduled for a Broadway opening before the year's end. The main thread of *Fancy Free* was retained. Three young sailors, on shore leave in Manhattan for twenty-four hours, are on the hunt for girls. But this idea was expanded into a complicated pattern. One of the sailors, Gaby, falls in love with the picture of "Miss Turnstiles" in the subway, a young lady by the name of Ivy. His two buddies, Ozzie and Chip, help him search for the living "Miss Turnstiles." They scour the city from Central Park to Coney Island, from Carnegie Hall to a night club, from Times Square to the Museum of Natural History. During this quest, Ozzie and Chip find girls of their own. Chip comes upon a female taxi driver, Claire, and Ozzie finds a young anthropology student, Hildy, at the Museum of Natural History. They all continue to seek out "Miss Turnstiles," until they come upon her in a Carnegie Hall studio, where she is taking vocal lessons.

Jerome Robbins, creator of the basic story line of *Fancy Free,* as well as its choreography, was recruited to devise the dance sequences. This was the first of many similarly significant assignments he would henceforth perform for the musical theater. George Abbott, one of the stage's most brilliant and successful directors, was willing to do the staging. Adolph Green and Betty Comden wrote text and lyrics and were cast in the parts of Ozzie and Claire. Sono Osato was engaged as "Miss Turnstiles" and Nancy Walker as Hildy. The musical comedy itself was baptized *On the Town.*

All concerned with it knew from the beginning that they were involved in a solid box-office attraction. Even before *On the Town* went into rehearsal, the motion-picture rights were sold to M-G-M for $100,000 plus a percentage of the gross receipts. When *On the Town* tried out in Boston, critics and audiences alike fell in love with it. For Bernstein, however, Boston provided a sobering antidote to all the infectious excitement and exhilaration generated by a successful play. For three hours, one evening, Koussevitzky took him severely to task for squandering his time, energy, and talent on pop tunes.

On the Town opened at the Adelphi Theater on December 28, 1944. In every department it had the exuberance, breeziness, gusto, and impudence of youth. George Abbott's staging and direction maintained a breathless pace and feeling of excitement from opening curtain to closing. *"On the Town,"* said *Time* Magazine, "sings and dances and joshes its way . . . [and] wherever it goes, uptown or down, it shoves dullness off the curbstone." In *The New York Times,* Lewis Nichols described it as "one of the freshest musicals to come into town in a long time."

Bernstein's music had the same kind of raciness, wit, and dynamic drive that vitalized the dialogue, lyrics, acting, and staging. For one now writing his first Broadway score he showed remarkable resiliency and adaptability in meeting the demands of lyrics and text. He could produce haunting ballads with a fine feeling for a well-sounding tune and a poignant emotion, as in "Lucky to Be Me" and "Lonely Town." His touch could suddenly become light and facetious in comic numbers like "I Get Carried Away" and "I Can Cook." He could write a highly atmospheric jazz number in "New York, New York." And a symphonic dimension—rich and inventive in its harmonic and instrumental vocabulary but without loss of popular inflections—could be found in his background music for the dance sequences.

In the year 1944 Bernstein became for Broadway a new, striking voice—a consummate musician who brought to popular writing a skill, taste, range of style, and an exciting freshness and originality not often encountered in the musical-comedy theater of that period. This music was so good that even fourteen years or so later it still proved an exciting experience. In 1959, Brooks Atkinson could say of this score: "Mr. Bernstein's tunes are certainly better—much, much better—than any that have been produced for Broadway this season."

Its Broadway run of 463 performances put it solidly in the hit class. But the history of *On the Town* did not end here. In 1949, M-G-M released the thoroughly entertaining motion-picture adaptation which starred Gene Kelly, Frank Sinatra, Ann Miller, and Betty Garrett. A decade after that two off-Broadway revivals took place simultaneously—one at the De Witt Clinton Adult Center, and the second at the Carnegie Hall Playhouse. "As it happens," said Walter Kerr in the New York *Herald Tribune* after witnessing one of these revivals, "I missed the original Broadway production of *On the Town,* and it wasn't until last evening . . . that I quite realized how unlucky I'd been. Fourteen years and a lot of good shows later, this . . . confection still stands as one of the most original, inventive, and irresistibly charming of all American musicals."

CHAPTER 10

"Lenny"

Up to the moment of his debut in 1943, Bernstein had been interviewed only once—then only by a youngster representing the Hunter High School magazine. One year after his debut there was hardly a newspaper or magazine in the entire country that had not publicized his already fantastic career as a "triple-note man of music," as *The New York Times* Magazine now described him. His picture graced the front cover of *Harper's Bazaar* and other national circulation magazines. He was quoted on every possible facet of his life, and on every conceivable musical subject.

His weekly mail was now in excess of five hundred letters. His telephone rarely stopped ringing—calls from agents of all sorts, journalists, and free-lance writers seeking interviews, young musicians seeking guidance and help, unknown admirers expressing enthusiasm. Bobby-soxers stopped him in the street for autographs, or crowded around him in wide-eyed adulation, as if he were Frank Sinatra. The U.S. Junior Chamber of Commerce named him one of the outstanding young men of 1944, together with the novelist, John Hersey, and the business tycoon (and later Governor of New York), Nelson A. Rockefeller.

Bernstein was deluged with offers. Symphony orchestras throughout the country sought him out for guest appearances, since he was now box-office magic. Tommy Dorsey wanted him to write original compositions and make arrangements for his band. Radio producers called him for coast-to-coast broadcasts; his wit and wisdom made him a favorite guest on the popular radio-quiz program, "Information Please." Paramount Pictures had him take a screen test with the hope of starring him in a screen biography of Tschaikovsky. Warner Brothers was considering him for its movie based on the life of George Gershwin. A few years later, a third Hollywood studio became interested in having him write scenario and music and play the piano for, besides acting in, a screen adaptation of Oliver Onions' *The Beckoning Fair One*. Most of these offers did not interest him. Those that did brought him an annual income in excess of $100,000.

He was forced to seek a larger apartment, finding it on the top floor of an old house in Washington Square. He also had to engage a secretary to handle his mail, answer the telephone, budget his time, arrange his appointments, protect him from well-meaning intruders, keep his scrapbooks. Fortunately, Helen Coates, his one-time piano teacher but now a close friend, was willing to come down from Boston, settle in New York, and take over a grueling assignment which since then she has been handling with the utmost grace and competence. (When Bernstein published his book, *The Joy of Music,* in 1959, he dedicated it "affectionately" to her "with deep appreciation for fifteen selfless years.")

"I couldn't believe that all this was happening to me," he confided to his friends. "I didn't really believe it was me at all. *Me* —a celebrity!"

He *was* a celebrity now, American music's matinee idol. And the casting was ideal. If Bernstein had been born to be a great musician, he had also been generously endowed by nature with those physical and personal attributes calculated to win friends and influence people. Off the podium, as on it, he made a striking impression. He stood five feet eight and a half inches, physically well developed, with powerful shoulders and the chest of an athlete. His handsome, leonine face combined strength and sensitivity: strength, in the vigorous profile, jutting jaw, burning intensity of the eyes; sensitivity, in the delicate curve of the lips, and in the mobile, expressive face that eloquently reflected his ever-changing moods. His unruly black hair—with a heavy shock hanging casually over an ample forehead—gave further accentuation to his "matinee idol" appeal. In time the temples and hair would be flecked with gray to contribute to his boyishness an impressive touch of dignity. He was always proud of his hair. He never wore a hat. At frequent intervals he would pass his hand hurriedly through the thick mane, or pass a comb swiftly through it to smooth its unruly waves.

He looked younger than his years, but there were many things about him that were adult and mature. His attitude to his work, art, and career was from the beginning both sober and professional. He had a fierce, intransigent integrity which refused to tolerate sham or hypocrisy of any kind, however expedient it might have been for him at any given moment to make compromises. His intelligence was expansive and penetrating. He could speak several languages quite well (French, Spanish, Italian, and Yiddish); of others (Hebrew and Latin) he had a smattering. His fund of information about a wide variety of subjects was remarkable, gained from extensive reading in many areas. When he appeared over the radio on the "Information Please" program he continually amazed radio listeners with the rich fund of his extramusical knowledge. In literature his tastes were sophisticated. They ranged from poetry (which he liked to write as well as read, and for which he had a genuine creative gift), and fiction, to biography, philosophy, and the classics. He had more than a passing acquaintance with metaphysics, philosophy, psychology, esthetics, the theater, the movies, current events. The spongelike tissues of his memory seemed to absorb everything and anything with which it came into contact. "If we wanted some ancient song, lyric, or routine we'd forgotten," says Adolph Green, "we just called up Lenny. He's our filing system. He might be hip-deep in Brahms, but he'll rattle off that song, first syllable to last, without a second's hesitation." He was always vitally concerned over the world about him, a belligerent liberal in politics, a progressive in his social viewpoints.

But much of his charm lay in the fact that despite all his sobriety and maturity he remained in many other ways a boy. A tendency toward exhibitionism, which he continually betrayed, had about it the disarming attitude of a school kid trying to impress a teacher. Few things delighted him more than discussing philosophy with philosophers, psychoanalysis with analysts, poetry with poets, stagecraft with people from the theater, and even cooking with chefs—and then notice their amazement at discovering how well informed he was in their own specialized fields. His outpouring of enthusiasms, his perpetual state of visible excitement about many different things, his exuberance, his seemingly inexhaustible vitality belong to youth rather than the mature. The same thing is true of his dogmatic opinions, and his healthy ego. He could say with conviction "I'm the logical man to write the great American opera" or "I can play this piece of music better than anybody" without sounding either brash or impudent or offensive. One naturally tolerates excessive self-evaluation and ingenuousness in the very young who are very gifted.

Inside the concert hall he might be the young Toscanini. Outside he was "Joe College." He dressed in more or less Ivy League fashion—casually, informally, and yet with an occasional touch of flamboyance. As soon as he could afford to do so, he indulged his interest in good clothes freely and took inordinate pride in his tailor. He often dragged along his friends to fittings which came to be known as "Lenny's dress rehearsals." He spoke with a Harvard accent—in a well-modulated voice that was precise in diction, and especially meticulous in the pronunciation of foreign terms. And yet, like so many collegiates, he liked to spice his talk with refreshing colloquialisms, Broadway jargon, plain slang, and figures of speech that revealed he knew something about boxing, baseball, or football. He had some of the penchants and interests of young collegiates. He was apt in sports (later on these included sailing and water-skiing); he was fond of the "funnies" (particularly Dick Tracy); and he was so crazy about the movies that he indiscriminately saw both the bad and the good and heartily enjoyed them all. Though a maestro of the redoubtable New York Philharmonic or the Boston Symphony, he never concealed the fact that he had a lifelong passion for jazz, show tunes, boogie-woogie; indeed, it was not at all unusual for him at rehearsals of symphony concerts to entertain the men of his orchestra with such music at the piano. He liked to do the samba and conga. He had a schoolboy's delight in games—chess, anagrams, double acrostics, crossword puzzles, charades. He enjoyed playing with kids; in their presence he became one of them. This uncommon gift for reaching out to youngsters and communicating with them on their own level was a gift he later used to wonderful advantage in making music for or in talking about music to young people. He often perpetrated little jokes, was glib with puns, and enjoyed the wit of his friends as much as he did his own. One of his little sports was to make up melodies which translated the telephone numbers of his friends into tones by having each number and letter of the dial telephone assume a specific musical value.

Unlike so many other musicians he was no introvert, but a highly social and gregarious person who loved parties and thrived on being with the people he liked. "I'm made for people, I love people, that's my weakness," he has confessed. He even liked having them near him when he was at work. Whoever came into contact with him reacted so strongly to his personal warmth and capacity for friendship that any kind of formal relationship seemed impossible. Even after he had become world-famous, all those who knew him socially or professionally spoke of him naturally as "Lenny"; any other form of address would have seemed to them false, pretentious, and outright affectation. When Bernstein became the music director of the New York Philharmonic the men of the orchestra held a meeting to decide on the correct way to speak to him. Some insisted that as music director he must henceforth be spoken to as "Mr. Bernstein," while some held out for "Maestro." But most of the men insisted that he had always been and always will be for them just "Lenny." A few of the more proper members of the orchestra later tried to compromise by addressing him as "Maestro Lenny" since they, too, felt that "Maestro" or "Mr. Bernstein" would not be suitable. But to all the others he remained— "Lenny."

CHAPTER II

"An artist has the compulsion to work"

Once again he had to ask himself: "Whither, Lenny?" In a way, this question was even more unsettling, more difficult to answer, than it had been in 1942. Three years earlier —as a failure who had confronted only dead-end streets wherever he turned—the choice in music had not been his to make. He was an innocent pawn in the hands of chance, or luck, or destiny, or whatever else one may wish to call that force that carries a man to his fulfillment. But in 1945 Bernstein was a recognized success in everything to which he had thus far put a hand. This decision was his, and his alone, as to which of several fields he should henceforth cultivate. Should he concentrate on being a conductor or a serious composer? Should he continue writing popular music for the Broadway stage? Should he develop his talent as pianist further?

Koussevitzky was not the only one to disapprove of the way he had begun to scatter his energies; who felt that this was the time in his career for him to devote himself more intensively to study, practice, and experimentation, and thereby develop himself more fully as a serious musician. Many of his friends insisted he was spreading himself too thin. Greatness in music, as elsewhere, comes only from specialization, from complete dedication to a single direction. What was it that Rachmaninoff had once said on reviewing his own career as composer, conductor, and pianist? "If you hunt three hares at once how sure can you be that you will kill one of them?"

Bernstein was far too astute and self-critical not to recognize the validity of these and similar arguments. Analyzing them in relation to his own career he underwent a considerable amount of soul searching and self-evaluation. He was still young, and he knew there was still a great deal for him to learn. He recognized the need for considerable more background and experience which could come only through hard work, and preferably hard work within a single area.

Despite his youth he had sufficient maturity and wisdom to accept the lavish acclaim already heaped on him without having his head turned or losing perspective. "There is only one thing for me to do," he said soberly in discussing his newly won triumphs, "and that is to forget everything—except my work." He did not fail to realize that his fame carried with it the awesome responsibility of having to give his audiences at all times the best that was in him.

Yet in his music he found it ever so difficult to contain himself, to curtail his varied endeavors, to stop penetrating into every possible direction. To work in a single facet of music to the exclusion of all others would have meant for him to function on a single cylinder both as a man and an artist. Perhaps one reason for this was his uninhibited passion for all kinds of music. He used to say, "music gives me the goosepimples." When he read a new score he was seized by the compulsion to carry this music from his inner ear to life in performance. When he browsed through a piano concerto he was helplessly driven to the piano to communicate his ideas about this composition to whoever would listen. To fail to express himself in this way would have resulted in an inner emptiness he could not suffer. In the same way, if an idea for a serious composition—or if his imagination was stimulated by some exciting project for the popular stage—

he felt smothered unless he could sit down and pinpoint his ideas on paper. "An artist has the compulsion to work," he insisted. "He'd go crazy if he didn't. I love my work—all of it." He simply had to communicate in every branch of music that fascinated him. His unique problem was that, unlike so many other musicians, he was fascinated by every single branch of music.

He decided to turn a deaf ear to all well-intentioned advice and criticism that insisted he canalize his talent through a single artery. He would function in the way his versatility, enthusiasm, and inner drives demanded. Such was his physical and nervous make-up that he thrived on the diversity of his undertakings. He seemed to have an almost inexhaustible reservoir of energy, vitality, and zest. Music never tired him. He could maintain a pace of activity that might exhaust anyone else; at the point where others might become vitiated, he would first begin to increase his momentum with a renewed burst of energy. After hours upon hours of hard work on one project he would be so ebullient, wide-eyed, and fresh that he could immediately embark on another task. Taking on a musical job completely different in character from one already completed was for him a revitalizing force. He explains: "Shifting from one thing to another is my vacation. I never get tired of working."

Not only did he have the capacity to progress from one assignment to the next almost before (so to speak) he caught his breath. He also had the capacity to work on several different assignments simultaneously, to operate on several different levels at once with a maximum capacity on each. One writer once remarked that it was almost as if Bernstein's brain had several different compartments, each able to handle a different task.

However much he diversified his activities, he knew that his main energy would have to be directed toward conducting. And in this sphere he achieved world-wide recognition within three years of his debut.

After a single season as assistant conductor of the New York Philharmonic, he resigned this post in the fall of 1944 to enlarge the scope of his conducting activity. He was called on to serve as a guest conductor of most of America's leading symphony orchestras. In the early part of 1945 he led the Boston Symphony (in Boston and Providence), the Pittsburgh Symphony, the New York Philharmonic, the St. Louis Symphony, and the Vancouver Symphony in British Columbia. During the summer he appeared at the Lewisohn Stadium in New York.

In the fall of 1945, Bernstein was appointed music director of the New York City Symphony. This was New York's youngest orchestra—founded in 1944 at the invitation of Mayor Fiorello La Guardia, with Leopold Stokowski as permanent conductor. Though this orchestra operated on a small budget—its survival made possible only because the conductor drew no salary and the players received a minimum wage—it had already become a vital part of the city's musical life.

Under Bernstein, its artistic significance grew by leaps and bounds. Once its director, he proceeded to reorganize it, replacing the weaker players with young, energetic, talented musicians. He set up a ten-week fall season with a duplicate series of concerts on Monday and Tuesday evenings. He tried to make his programs continually provocative and exciting with innovations, premières, and revivals. He introduced new works by many Americans, including Vernon Duke, Alex North, and Marc Blitzstein among others. He gave the first American performance in a dozen years of Béla Bartók's *Music for Strings, Percussion, and Celesta,* a modern masterwork. And after an equally long period of neglect, Blitzstein's controversial opera *The Cradle Will Rock,* and Alban Berg's exciting expressionist opera *Wozzeck* were revived, both of them in concert versions, and the latter through salient excerpts. Hindemith, Milhaud, Chávez, Copland, Stravinsky were some of the masters of 20th-century music represented on Bernstein's programs. An all-Stravinsky program included the rarely heard opera-oratorio *Oedipus Rex.* An all-British concert traversed the centuries from Purcell to Benjamin Britten. An all-Mozart performance included a piano concerto which Bernstein played while conducting the accompaniment. There was a continual feeling of adventure about these concerts that made it impossible for the New York City Symphony audiences to lapse into complacency.

While holding this office of music director, Bernstein continued to make important appearances elsewhere. In the spring of 1946 he was invited to conduct two concerts of American music at an international festival in Prague, Czechoslovakia, commemorating the fiftieth anniversary of the Czech Philharmonic. Though Sir Thomas Beecham and Charles Munch also appeared there as representatives of their respective countries, it was Bernstein who, in the opinion of several correspondents, stole the limelight. On May 15 his program included William Schuman's *American Festival Overture,* Samuel Barber's *Essay No. 2,* George Gershwin's *Rhapsody in Blue* (Eugene List, soloist), Roy Harris' Symphony No. 3, and Copland's *El Salón México.* On May 16 Bernstein repeated the program except for the substitution of his own *Jeremiah Symphony* for the Gershwin rhapsody. On each occasion he brought down the house. The high standards set both by his performance, and the music he presented, provided a powerful testimony to Europe that musical America was finally coming of age.

That summer, on August 6, Bernstein conducted at Tanglewood the American première of one of the most significant operas of the 20th century, Benjamin Britten's *Peter Grimes.* That opera had been commissioned by the Koussevitzky Foundation, and its world première in London a year earlier (June 7, 1945) had proved a sensation. Bernstein's dynamic, searching performance gave *Peter Grimes* an impressive American send-off.

Among the important American orchestras conducted by Bernstein during the regular winter seasons between 1946 and 1948 were the Boston Symphony, the NBC Symphony, the Cincinnati Symphony, the Rochester Philharmonic, the St. Louis Symphony, the Houston Symphony, and the Minneapolis Symphony. In 1947 he directed two of the regular festival programs of the Boston Symphony at Tanglewood—the first time Koussevitzky allowed anyone but himself to conduct these concerts.

Bernstein's fame as conductor circled half the world in 1947 when he embarked on his first tour of the Near East and Europe. His first appearance with the Palestine Philharmonic early that year was probably the greatest personal triumph he had thus far enjoyed. Only a small fraction of those who wanted to hear the concert could get into the auditorium—even though the aisles and the rear of the auditorium were crowded with standees three-deep. At this Near East debut Bernstein conducted his *Jeremiah Symphony,* the orchestral parts of which, shipped from New York, were lost somewhere en route to Palestine. A hurried call for a duplicate set brought them to Palestine just three days before concert time.

The excitement generated by Bernstein's performance mounted with each number until the final outburst resembled pandemonium. "He is one of the most talked of personalities and popular visitors in years," reported Peter Gradenwitz to *The New York Times.* "The enthusiasm of the audience at his first concert with the Philharmonic Orchestra knew no bounds, and not since the days of Arturo Toscanini—who, as you will remember, launched our orchestra on its way ten years ago—has a conductor been recalled so many times and given a similar ovation." Then Mr. Gradenwitz went on to report that the Philharmonic "has never been better. Its . . . musicians were

89

fascinated by Mr. Bernstein, the conductor and pianist; and measuring their enthusiasm, we should not forget that the orchestra has played under Toscanini, Weingartner, Molinari, Sargent, Szenkar, Steinberg, and Munch. The concerts with Mr. Bernstein were the climax of the orchestra's tenth season."

After that, Bernstein appeared at the second International Festival in Prague, and in Germany, Austria, France, Belgium, and The Netherlands. In London he gave four programs, on each of which he featured at least one American or British composition. In Scheveningen, Holland, he gave an exciting demonstration of his versatility to achieve once again a personal success of the first magnitude. Nathan Milstein, the violin virtuoso, had been scheduled to appear as soloist on Bernstein's program. Because of a French railway strike, Milstein was unable to reach Holland. At the last moment, Bernstein substituted for Milstein by playing and conducting the Ravel G major Concerto to the delight, and awe, of his audience.

CHAPTER 12

"When I'm conducting, nothing else exists"

Just before the opening of Bernstein's third season as musical director of the New York City Symphony he attended a dinner at which a city official pointed with civic pride to the fact that New York was "supporting" such a fine musical organization. From his seat Bernstein shouted out: "Fraud!"

This was not the first time he was put out by the prevailing misconception that the city was paying the bills for his orchestra. The cold truth was that New York contributed nothing whatsoever toward its maintenance. The seasonal deficit of about $50,000 was made up from profits derived from other attractions at the New York City Center. In addition, in 1947 the American Federation of Musicians contributed a subsidy of $10,000. Even so, the musicians of the orchestra were woefully underpaid, while Bernstein himself drew no salary.

His shout of "fraud," however, was the first time Bernstein made his feelings so public. It helped to dramatize in the newspapers the highly precarious existence of this distinguished musical organization. In 1948, the American Federation of Musicians announced it would not contribute a second subsidy of $10,000 for the coming season. The loss of this sorely needed additional income represented a death blow to Bernstein's plans for his orchestra. He firmly announced his resignation. "Rather than a reduction in the budget," he wrote in explanation to the director of the City Center, "I had for three years been looking forward to an expansion, which I feel is now necessary. By expansion I mean an increase in the number of concerts given (with resultant increase in financial security of the orchestra members), an increase in the size of the orchestra, and an increase in the length of the season. While it is reasonable to expect the usual 10% increase in ticket sales (in line with the steadily mounting attendance records) this would not be enough to guarantee the 1948 season, even with no expansion at all. I have, therefore, tendered my resignation with reluctance and sadness."

A few months later an announcement explained that differences between the orchestral management and Bernstein had finally been resolved harmoniously. But since the time was now late for planning the 1948 season, it would be completely eliminated, with operations resumed under Bernstein after a year's hiatus. Actually nothing of the sort happened. The money Bernstein insisted his orchestra needed was never found. When he refused to reassume his post in 1949, the orchestra passed out of existence.

For about another decade, Bernstein was without an orchestra of his own, but, of course, he was not without orchestras. During the next few years he bestrode the world of music with seven league boots. There was hardly an important symphonic organization anywhere in Europe, the Near East, as well as the United States, that did not call him for performances. Whenever he came abroad he brought with him works of American composers, for he had by now become an eloquent spokesman and the passionate propagandist for the musical culture of his native land. He also performed the music of Europeans, old and new, a graceful gesture of his respect to the Old World he was visiting. He conducted English composers in Great Britain,

Robert Schumann in Germany, Béla Bartók in Hungary, Cherubini in Milan.

In 1948 he gave his first command performance. This took place in Amsterdam. The pleasure of performing before royalty was undoubtedly a keen one. But it is more than probable that another of his European concerts that year afforded him even profounder satisfaction. In Munich, Germany—once the hotbed of Nazism, once the scene of the most virulent anti-Semitic demonstrations—he performed and received an ovation for a Hebraic composition, his own *Jeremiah Symphony*.

In 1950, his cyclonic performance of Mahler's Second Symphony at the Holland Music Festival was described by one of the local critics as a "revelation"—this in a city where for many years Willem Mengelberg's interpretations of Mahler with the Concertgebouw Orchestra had been regarded by the rest of the world as the ultimate criterion. In 1953, Bernstein's first appearance at La Scala in Milan—where he led performances of Cherubini's *Medea* with Maria Callas in the title role—represented the first time in the long and eventful history of that opera house that an American-born conductor appeared during the regular season.

If Bernstein was to be deprived of the luxury of having an orchestra of his own all through these years, there were at least two symphonic organizations (other than the New York Philharmonic) that were particularly close to his heart. One was the Boston Symphony—Koussevitzky's orchestra; the orchestra of the Berkshire Music Festival; the orchestra of Bernstein's home city; the first orchestra he had ever heard play. February 18, 1944, when he conducted the Boston Symphony for the first time, had been an occasion overflowing with sentiment as far as he was concerned. He was no longer the native son returning home with "tail between my knees," but the conquering hero—rhapsodized in the Boston newspapers with feature stories and cheered by the audiences at Symphony Hall. As he walked the streets of Boston, which conjured up to him more than one image of past defeats, he could savor the full sweet taste of his success. That exhilaration, and that sense of personal victory, may have lost some of its edge with his later appearances in Boston. But he never lost his pleasure—sentimental as well as musical—in conducting the Boston Symphony. Koussevitzky gave him plenty of opportunities to do so—not only in Boston but even in New York and Brooklyn, something Koussevitzky permitted no other conductor to do. Koussevitzky also allowed Bernstein to indulge his passion for modern music freely at the Boston Symphony concerts. He presented significant world premières. Some were by young Americans (for example, Harold Shapero's *Symphony for Classical Orchestra*); some were by established Americans (David Diamond's Symphony No. 4); some even by distinguished Europeans (Olivier Messiaen's mammoth ten-movement apotheosis of rhythm, *Turangalîla*). Bernstein performed a considerable number of other modern works, among them Stravinsky's *The Rite of Spring,* Hindemith's Violin Concerto, Copland's *El Salón México,* and Charles Ives' Symphony No. 2. (The last of these works had been written between 1897 and 1902. But it had to wait half a century—and for Leonard Bernstein—before it received its world première, at a concert of the New York Philharmonic on February 22, 1951.)

Though Koussevitzky retired as music director of the Boston Symphony in 1949, to be succeeded by Charles Munch, Bernstein's association with that orchestra did not end. He continued to make many welcome appearances with that orchestra, both in and out of Boston.

A second orchestra with which Bernstein has always maintained a strong emotional bond since 1947 was the Palestine Philharmonic. When the State of Israel was established in 1948, the name of the orchestra was changed to Israel Philharmonic. Soon after this change of name took place, Bernstein announced he would accept the post of music director. The assumption of this office, for one reason or another, did not prove feasible to him, but he nevertheless made frequent guest appearances with the orchestra and for a while even served as its "musical adviser." In the fall of 1948 he led the Israel Philharmonic in forty concerts in a sixty-day period in Tel Aviv, Jerusalem, Haifa, Rehoboth, and Beersheba, often appearing in the dual capacity of conductor and pianist. At Beersheba he led the first symphony concert ever heard in that ancient Biblical city; an open-air performance which included Gershwin's *Rhapsody in Blue* had been arranged there for the benefit of Israeli soldiers who had come from many miles around to hear the performance.

Bernstein won the love and admiration of all Israelis, not merely for his genius as a conductor but also for his demonstrations of personal courage. At that time Israel was involved in continual open fighting with the Arabs. In their tour of Israel, Bernstein and his orchestra were often only forty-eight hours behind Israeli troops. The musicians passed roads to Galilee lined with the bodies of dead Arabs. With many of Bernstein's concerts taking place within range of the shooting, the music on more than one occasion was accompanied by an obligato of shell explosions. If Bernstein felt any discomfort or anxiety, being so close to the firing range, he failed to reveal this either during his concerts or in his personal associations with the Israelis. At a concert in Rehoboth an air-raid alarm was sounded while Bernstein was playing and conducting a Beethoven concerto. He later confessed that he suspected that "this was my swan song." But he kept on playing and conducting as if his performance were taking place under the most ideal conditions. When not participating at formal concerts, Bernstein appeared at military camps and hospitals to entertain their occupants with his piano playing. Such dedication to the people and the country did not go unrecognized. Before leaving Israel, Bernstein received the decoration of the Emblem of the Defenders of Jerusalem as two thousand Israeli soldiers stood and cheered.

Bernstein has maintained an intimate relationship with the Israel Philharmonic both in and out of Israel. When, early in 1951, the orchestra made its first tour of the United States, the conductor's dais was shared by Bernstein and Koussevitzky. Over a 2-month period, Bernstein directed 12 concerts during a nationwide journey that covered 40 cities and included some 55 performances in all. This American tour was officially launched with a dinner at the Waldorf-Astoria Hotel in New York, on January 8, 1951, the highlight of which was a concert by the Israel Philharmonic under Bernstein's direction.

Then, in 1955, The Israel Philharmonic undertook an extensive European tour over an 8-week period, with 43 concerts in 9 countries. And once again Bernstein was one of its principal conductors.

When, on October 2, 1957, a new concert hall was opened in Tel Aviv—the Frederick R. Mann Auditorium—with a gala concert by the Israel Philharmonic and with Artur Rubinstein, Gregor Piatigorsky, and Isaac Stern as soloists, the conductor above all others called on to direct this historic event was Leonard Bernstein.

Bernstein, then, has captured the heart, the mind, and the imagination of the world with his remarkable musicianship and his equally commanding personality.

As a conductor, Bernstein is a technician of the highest order. Nature has been bountiful to him by endowing him with a fabulous ear and memory. In addition, his instinctive and innate musical intelligence provides him with an articulateness that enables him to read, speak, and think in musical terms as easily as in verbal ones. In conducting music, however abstruse or esoteric, he knows it to its slightest markings of each page. He understands the technical demands made by it on himself and his men, the printed page never holding any problems for him. He knows how he wants the music to sound. But equally important in making him a great conductor is his compelling personal appeal and his rare gift of communication.

At rehearsals some conductors are veritable tyrants, achieving their best results from the men through displays of violent temper and the exercise of dictatorial power. Toscanini, Stokowski, Koussevitzky were all like that. Other conductors manage to create a warm, human relationship between themselves and their orchestra. That is the way Bernstein likes to work. At rehearsals, as away from them, he is "Lenny" rather than "the Maestro." What he wants from the musicians he manages to get through his powers of logic, friendly persuasion, and a high regard for each man's dignity and self-respect. He likes to lighten and relax the tense atmosphere of rigorous rehearsals with light banter and slang. "Next four bars," he might say, "square, *sehr* square!" He will mimic, make puns, go into droll pantomime. Sometimes he may indulge in an analysis of the inner meaning of some piece of music. Sometimes he tries to arouse the men through uninhibited emotional demonstrations as the music is being played. He swoons, prays, scowls, fumes, entreats, sings. He is not afraid to voice his boyish enthusiasms. "This music simply *slays me!*" he once shouted after a particularly beautiful passage had been played. But by the time his rehearsal is over he has managed to get his message across.

His ear, memory, articulateness, and capacity to transmit to his men his every artistic demand clearly and precisely are some of the qualities that made it possible for him to become one of the world's great conductors in such a short period of time. It takes many, many years for any conductor to acquire a working repertory, especially if, like Bernstein, he is acutely aware of his responsibilities to his contemporaries and to the music they are writing. Most conductors get that repertory (as well as their conducting know-how) by fulfilling a rigorous apprenticeship with a small orchestra of a minor city. Away from the limelight of national or world attention these conductors can go through their growing pains as artists until they arrive at assurance as technicians and maturity as musicians. Bernstein never had that apprenticeship. From his New York Philharmonic debut on he was always called on to conduct the world's greatest orchestras in the most exacting programs. In his first years as conductor there were many works in the standard repertory he had never studied, let alone performed. In presenting these works for the first time he was the center of national or world interest—not an obscure apprentice functioning in some out-of-the-way town. With his very first presentation of each of these masterworks his conception and interpretation were measured by the yardstick of performances by the world's foremost conductors—each of whom had played, digested, and studied the same works a lifetime.

This was a serious handicap for Bernstein to overcome. It might have proved fatal. But Bernstein hurdled it gracefully because of his phenomenal capacity to learn new scores quickly; because of his facility in unraveling technical complexities; because of his sure instincts in understanding what a composer is trying to say; and because of his natural aptitude as a born teacher in passing on instruction to the orchestra. Thus he was able to fulfill his world-wide commitments even while he was building his own repertory.

Together with his natural endowments as a musician, he has been blessed with a personality able to arouse, excite, inflame both the orchestra and the audiences. The intensity, the exaltation, and the passion he feels about every piece of music he conducts make themselves strongly felt as soon as he starts to conduct it. During the actual performance, these emotions find expression in his platform behavior. On the conductor's stand Bernstein is a visual as well as an aural experience. Not only hands, but even head, body, and knees respond to the emotional impact of the music, almost as if each had a will and a response of its own. He throws his fists angrily into the air; he sinks to the floor in humble supplication; he raises his face and arms heavenward in exaltation; he stands immobile and transfixed as his left hand quivers near his heart. At one time Virgil Thomson described him as "our musical Dick Tracy. . . . He shagged, shimmied and believe it or not bumped." Bernstein explains: "I honestly don't realize what I'm doing on the podium. When I'm conducting, nothing else exists but the music."

A fiery temperament that invites such highly subjective reactions to music is, to be sure, better in some types of music than in others. Bernstein is usually more at ease, and more effective, in works with hyperthyroid tensions and emotional indulgences than he is in music of tight-lipped restraint and classic beauty. Bernstein has always been more exciting in performances of, say, Mahler's Second Symphony (the *Resurrection*), Liszt's *Faust Symphony,* Schumann's Second Symphony, or Brahms' First Symphony than he has been in Haydn or Mozart. But his artistic gamut is by no means a limited one. If the dynamic impact of his presentations of Romantic and post-Romantic music has been arrestingly dramatic and emotional, he has also demonstrated a remarkable empathy with such old masters as Bach, Handel, and Beethoven. It takes a good deal of living, a good deal of thought and background, to translate the musical sounds of Bach or Beethoven into human experience. Such a profound human experience is beginning to assert itself more and more strongly in Bernstein's conceptions of masterworks like the *Eroica* and the Ninth Symphonies and the *Missa Solemnis,* all by Beethoven. This is due to the fact that Bernstein's musical genius is a partner to his rich and varied culture. Well read and well informed as he is in so many fields, he possesses that depth of intellectual understanding—that *Weltanschauung*—necessary for uncovering in the music of the masters the extra-musical meanings and aspirations of their most subtle or penetrating thoughts.

99

But if there is any single area in which Bernstein is not only at his best but in some respects unique, it is in the music of the moderns. He is a child of his times, and he is its voice. The complex, nervous, often discordant sounds of the modern composer is an idiom that comes as naturally to him as little colloquialisms and Americanisms do to his speech. Through the speech of the moderns, Bernstein seems best able to express his own dynamic, turbulent personality. In works by Stravinsky, Copland, Bartók, Shostakovich, Prokofiev, and the younger Americans, Bernstein is unquestionably one of the outstanding musical interpreters of our generation.

CHAPTER 13

"The only way one can really say anything about music is to write music"

While Leonard Bernstein was freely roaming the world directing its leading orchestras and appearing at its principal festivals, he was not idle as a composer.

The year 1946 saw the première of a second Bernstein ballet: *Facsimile,* a production of the Ballet Theater, choreography by Jerome Robbins. The first performance took place at the Broadway Theater in New York on October 24, the composer conducting. *Facsimile* was an allegory about the emptiness in the lives of so many people today. To point up this problem, the program quoted a motto by Ramon y Cajal: "Small inward treasure does he possess who, to feel alive, needs every hour the tumult of the street, the emotion of the theater, and the small talk of society."

The ballet had only three characters: The Woman, The Man, Another Man. The Woman stands alone on a desolate beach trying to amuse herself as best she can. She plays with her shadow, she dances about, she toys with an object in her hand. First one man, then the second, arrives and tries to attract her interest. The first man bores her, but she becomes more stimulated when the second one presents himself as a rival to the first. The two men get embroiled in a bitter fight over her until she angrily brings it to a halt. The two men leave, frustrated. The girl once again is left alone on the beach trying to find distraction from boredom.

This ballet represented for Bernstein a radical change of pace from *Fancy Free*. His first ballet had been realistic and satirical, modern and racy. The second was melodramatic, atmospheric, at times nebulous. Ever resilient in adapting his musical style and thinking to the requirements of a text, Bernstein produced for *Facsimile* a score far different in texture and idiom from that for *Fancy Free*. In the latter, extensive use had been made of jazz and other popular styles within a witty, jaunty, sprightly score. In *Facsimile* Bernstein was the serious modernist, utilizing the fullest resources of contemporary writing in music that was gripping in dramatic impact and high-tensioned in mood.

Once again, almost as if further to demonstrate his creative flexibility, Bernstein wrote in 1947 a serious piece of music far different from *Facsimile*. This was a song cycle called *La Bonne cuisine* which (for all its technical complexities and subtleties of expression) was music of a light heart and gay spirit. Bernstein (himself a gourmet who was not without some skill in the kitchen) came upon an old French cookbook in a house he rented one summer in Tanglewood. He found inordinate delight in reading the recipes aloud as if they were poems; they stimulated his musical imagination. He finally set four of the recipes to appropriate music.

In 1948 he was hard at work on his second symphony. His inspiration came from a "baroque eclogue" by W. H. Auden, *The Age of Anxiety*. "The moment I finished reading this poem," Bernstein says, "the composition of a symphony acquired an almost compulsive quality." Despite the fact that he was almost always on the move, he could not let the symphony alone. He wrote parts in Taos (New Mexico), Philadelphia, Richmond, and Tel Aviv. The orchestration was done while he was making a month-long tour with the Pittsburgh Symphony. Scored for piano and orchestra, the symphony was completed on March 20, 1949. Below the last bar of the last page Bernstein scribbled: "NYC—the first day of Spring!" The world première took place soon after that—on April 8, 1949 in Boston. Serge Koussevitzky (to whom the work is dedicated) conducted the Boston Symphony, and Bernstein played the piano obbligato.

Like the poem on which it was based, Bernstein's music was, in the composer's own explanation, "a record of our difficult and problematical search for faith." Bernstein planned to use the poem only as a point of departure for his own musical thinking. He had originally had no desire to translate into literal musical terms both the programmatic content and the philosophic and social overtones of the eclogue. "Yet," says Bernstein, "when each section was finished I discovered upon rereading, detail after detail of programmatic relation to the poem —details that had 'written themselves,' wholly unplanned and unconscious."

The symphony is in two parts, each with subdivisions. The first, "The Seven Ages," consists of an introduction and fourteen variations. In the Introduction, four lonely characters (a girl and three men) are in a bar on New York's Third Avenue. Each is trying to escape from inner turmoil, conflicts, and doubts. Before long they are drawn to one another through the necessity of finding some common bond or urge. They begin discussing the state of man, "The Seven Ages." The first part of "The Seven Ages" (Variations 1 through 7) is a discussion of the life of man from the four personal points of view of each of the characters. In the next set of variations (8 through 14) the four characters embark on a symbolic journey in search of security.

The second part of the symphony has three divisions. "The

Dirge" places the four characters in a taxi enroute to the girl's apartment for a nightcap. Here they all bemoan their lack of a leader, or a "colossal Dad," someone to give them direction and leadership and serve as a kind of father-symbol. In "The Masque" the four characters are at the girl's apartment trying to forget their guilt and weariness. They then disperse. In the concluding "Epilogue" each is finally freed from guilt and able to find faith.

The Age of Anxiety is Bernstein's most complex and eclectic composition. With extreme skill and fluency he manages to find the proper style—the *mot juste*—for each mood, situation, or intellectual concept posed by Auden's poem. At times he employs jazz; at times the esoteric twelve-tone technique made famous by Arnold Schoenberg; at times an unashamedly Romantic effusion in the manner of Brahms; at times the welcome outpouring of pure melody; and at times the harsh discords and tonalities of the ultra modernist. Yet such is Bernstein's craftmanship that an artistic unity is created from these disparate idioms. Such are his creative gifts that he is able at all times to produce music of immense communicative power and deep poetic feeling. To Howard Taubman of *The New York Times,* this was "impressive . . . music . . . moving toward economy, simplicity, and clarity." Mr. Taubman goes on to say: "The opening section in its restraint and evocation of the mood, is particularly pat, and the Masque in the middle of the second part has a brilliant vitality. . . . The piece contains a dirge, written with resourcefulness, and an epilogue that makes its effect."

The Age of Anxiety was awarded the Hornblit Prize of $1,000 which each year is presented to the best new work heard at the concerts of the Boston Symphony. On February 26, 1950, a ballet inspired by this music—also named *The Age of Anxiety*—was produced by the New York City Ballet with choreography by Jerome Robbins.

The year 1951 brought Bernstein both tragedy and happiness. Tragedy came on June 24 with the death in Boston of Serge Koussevitzky. Koussevitzky had been his second father; his teacher, mentor, and inspiration all in one; the man probably most responsible for his successful development; the North Star by which he had been traveling in his career. Now Koussevitzky was gone. The gap left in Bernstein's life nobody else could hope to fill.

Bernstein was on vacation in Cuernavaca, Mexico, when Koussevitzky's wife phoned him from Boston to tell him how sick the Maestro was. Without bothering to pack a valise, Bernstein rushed to the airport and arrived in Boston twenty hours later. Thus he was able to spend Koussevitzky's last night with him.

But there was gain as well as loss that year. On September 9, 1951, Bernstein married Felicia Montealegre Cohn.

She had come to New York from Santiago, Chile. She had been born in Costa Rica on February 26, 1922—a slight, slender, petite, and beautiful girl with sensitive hazel eyes, a delicate mouth, a serene expression on her face, and a stately carriage. Her father, an American, was head of the American Smelting and Refining Company branch in Santiago. Felicia had come to New York with the hope of becoming an actress but her immediate purpose was to study the piano with her compatriot, the famous concert pianist, Claudio Arrau.

Soon after her arrival, a birthday party was given jointly for her and Arrau at the latter's home in Douglaston, Long Island. Bernstein was invited, and at the party he was introduced to Felicia. They were immediately drawn to each other. From then on they saw each other frequently. By the end of that year—1946—they announced their engagement.

Eventually both of them realized that, despite their mutual attachment, neither one was yet ready for marriage. Nine months after the announcement of their engagement, while Bernstein was in Prague, they finally decided on separation. During the next few years they saw each other only occasionally, and in passing. While Bernstein continued to pursue a nomadic existence around the world, Felicia was finally able to realize her lifelong ambition through several successful dramatic appearances on television.

Then, one evening in 1950, they met again at Shirley Bernstein's apartment. (Shirley, now also working in television, had all the while maintained contact with Felicia.) Leonard Bernstein and Felicia now took up where they had left off in 1947. At last they came to realize that whatever the hazards of marriage between two career people—and with one of them always on the go—their life apart could no longer be tolerated. One day, in the summer of 1951, while motoring to Tanglewood, they dropped off for lunch at an inn. There Bernstein proposed marriage to Felicia. They announced their second engagement in Tanglewood on August 12, 1951, at a faculty buffet supper of the Berkshire Music Center.

On September 9 they were married in Boston in a simple religious ceremony at Temple Mishkan Tefila where, as a boy, Bernstein had received religious instruction and where, in his thirteenth year, he had been confirmed. Only thirty-three guests were present—mainly close relatives and a few intimate friends.

The change in his personal life led Bernstein to reappraise his professional one. Once again the ever-vexing problem haunted him: Should he begin to specialize in a single field of music? He decided that this was the time for him to take stock of himself. The only way to do so was to go into seclusion for a year or so, to give himself both the time and the serenity with which to think things out soberly. As a matter of fact, he had been planning just such a Sabbatical when, earlier the same year, he had come to Mexico. Now that he was married he was determined to continue that Sabbatical where it had been interrupted by Koussevitzky's death. He rented a house again in Cuernavaca, Mexico, to which he escaped with his bride—his intention being to stay put indefinitely, withdrawn from all conducting commitments. He wanted to think and to compose music. He was planning an opera.

But this retirement once again proved short-lived. When Charles Munch suddenly fell ill in Boston, Bernstein was called on to substitute for him for several of the concerts of the Boston Symphony. The Mexican idyl thus came to an abrupt end. The main problem that beset Bernstein remained unanswered. But he did manage to finish his opera.

The opera was *Trouble in Tahiti,* an amusing, unconventional little domestic comedy in one act and seven scenes for which Bernstein wrote his own libretto. On June 12, 1952 it was given its first performance under the composer's direction at the Festival of the Creative Arts at Brandeis University in Waltham, Massachusetts (of which Bernstein was artistic director).

The libretto touched lightly on a subject which had previously been discussed so much more gravely and with such greater depth in *Facsimile* and the second symphony: the present-day loneliness and emptiness of many people. All this was symbolized in the opera in the daily trivial bickerings of a young married couple in a typical suburban community. After an unpleasant breakfast, in which angry words are exchanged, the husband goes off to town to attend to business and visit a gymnasium. The wife also comes to town, first to see her psychiatrist, and then to go to a movie called *Trouble in Tahiti.* When they meet at home again that evening, they resume the morning's little quarrels and misunderstanding. Finally, after the evening meal, they decide to flee from the unpleasantness of their home life by going to the local movie theater, which is showing *Trouble in Tahiti.*

Actually this is more like a revue skit than an opera. But the gaiety, verve, satirical overtones of Bernstein's music—

much of it in a jazz style, and some of it in the idiom of Tin Pan Alley—gave the opera cogency, humor, and appeal. "Mr. Bernstein," reported Howard Taubman, "writes with delicious and irresistible vitality." In the *Saturday Review,* Irving Kolodin described Bernstein's music as "crisp and flavorsome, even witty. . . . The strains designed to give credibility to the personal drama of the people involved are often inventive and, if not precisely moving, possessed of a kind of wistful poetry."

Trouble in Tahiti has been seen several times since its Waltham première. In the fall of 1952 it was given a production over television, and after that it was performed at Tanglewood. On April 19, 1955 it came to Broadway as part of a program entitled *All in One,* which included dances by Paul Draper and a one-act play by Tennessee Williams.

The dream of spending a year of quiet and seclusion in some Mexican Shangri-La remained just that—a dream. In 1952 Bernstein was once again helplessly sucked into the vortex of his many activities. With Koussevitzky gone, he had to take over the conducting and orchestra classes at Tanglewood during the summer. That same year he assumed the position of professor of music and director of the School of Creative Arts at Brandeis University in Waltham, which he held for five years. His conducting assignments were again sweeping him across the face of the map. In addition to all this, he was deep at work on his second Broadway musical comedy.

The decision to write another musical comedy had been made somewhat impetuously. One day, in 1952, Adolph Green and Betty Comden visited Bernstein. Since he was not at home they decided to wait for him, and while waiting they vigorously thrashed out a problem then uppermost in their minds. They had been asked to adapt for the musical-comedy stage the delightful stage comedy, *My Sister Eileen,* which in turn had been derived from stories which Ruth McKenney wrote

for and published in *The New Yorker*. What bothered them
first of all was a four-week deadline. If a musical comedy was
not completely written by then, Rosalind Russell, the Hollywood star who was interested in appearing in the production,
would no longer be available for it. They had a second concern, as well. Was *My Sister Eileen* too dated to become good
musical-comedy theater in 1952? "*Eileen* seemed so awfully
'Thirties bound," was the way Adolph Green put it, "a sort of
post-war depression play, full of overexploited plot lines and
passé references!"

They were so deep in discussion that they failed to notice
Bernstein standing in the doorway listening to them with rapt
interest. "The 'Thirties!" he finally shouted at them. "What a
wonderful period! What excitement there was in those days!
What wonderful songs!" Bernstein rushed to his piano and
began playing some of the popular show tunes of that era.
Suddenly he stopped, thought for a moment, and remarked:
"Here, I've got an idea for a show tune for *Eileen*. Listen."
And he began playing a melody that had just popped into his
head.

It was at that moment that Bernstein became one of the
collaborators on this new musical comedy, and it was also at
that moment that he, Green, and Comden started to work.
For the next month they practically lived in Bernstein's studio,
working feverishly on the lyrics and music for fourteen numbers
to a musical-comedy text named *Wonderful Town* already
prepared for them by Joseph Fields and Jerome Chodorov.
"We'd sit in Lenny's cave working until we couldn't see each
other for the smoke," recalls Betty Comden. "Whenever one
of the fourteen songs was finished, Bernstein would come in
saying, 'O.K., geniuses, let's hear it.' The show? We started
rehearsals right on schedule."

On February 25, 1953, *Wonderful Town* "roared into the
Winter Garden like a hurricane," as Robert Coleman wrote

in the *Mirror*. It became one of the most exciting and successful productions of that season, with a run of 553 performances.
It received the Drama Critics Award as the year's best musical
and Bernstein's score was honored with the Antoinette Perry
and Donaldson Awards. A national company toured the
country, and it was successfully produced in several European
capitals. On November 30, 1958 the show was televised on the
CBS network.

The setting of *Wonderful Town* was Greenwich Village, in
New York, in the 1930's. Two girls from Ohio have come seeking their fortune in the arts. One of them is Eileen (played
by Edith Adams), a baby-faced, baby-voiced innocent hoping
to get on the stage. The other is her sophisticated, somewhat
hard-boiled sister, Ruth (enacted by Rosalind Russell), aspiring
for a career as writer. As soon as they establish residence in a
basement apartment (under which a subway is being constructed) they are surrounded by a varied assortment of eccen-
trics and "squares." Eileen apparently attracts men with her
wide-eyed, open stare the way a magnet draws iron. An ex-
football star, a magazine editor, a night-club owner, a manager
of a 44th Street drugstore, and a newspaperman are some of
those haunting the basement apartment of the two girls. Eileen
and Ruth become helplessly involved in all kinds of adventures
and misadventures. Somewhere along the way, Eileen gets
arrested; and Ruth, sent by a prankster on a wild-goose newspaper assignment, gets embroiled in Brooklyn with the Bra-
zilian Navy. But in the end things come out well for both
girls. The publicity of her arrest gains Eileen a job in a night
club, while Ruth gets a position with a newspaper. Perhaps
even more important, both girls get the men of their hearts.

Directed by George Abbott, with the exuberance, uproar, and
split-second timing for which he had long become famous,
Wonderful Town never stopped to catch its breath. "From the
moment the curtain goes up on a rag-tag dance of Village

characters," wrote Brooks Atkinson, "one crack-brained crisis leads logically into another throughout a full evening of organized bedlam and insanity." The dynamo of the production was Rosalind Russell, who raced breathlessly through Ruth's role like an uncontrolled locomotive, gaining speed all the time, and seeming to be rushing to inevitable disaster. Her inexhaustible energy left audiences limp with emotion at the final curtain.

The excitement generated by George Abbott's direction and Rosalind Russell's performance could also be found in Bernstein's music. "In Leonard Bernstein," said Brooks Atkinson, "they have the perfect composer for this sort of work—a modern with a sense of humor and a gift of melody. . . . He writes with wit, scope, and variety." Every nuance of sentiment, satire, and broad burlesque captured by the dialogue and stage action vibrated as well in the remarkable score which traversed the scale of mood and emotion from exciting ragtime and swing music to romantic ballads. Of the latter, the best songs were "A Quiet Girl" and "Never Felt that Way." The music also embraced tongue-in-cheek parodies of an Irish ballad ("My Darlin' Eileen") and of songs about home ("Ohio"), as well as merry caricatures ("Pass that Football," "One Hundred Easy Ways," and "Story Vignettes").

The left hand might be writing popular music, but the right hand was still concerned creatively with sterner stuff. In 1954, Bernstein completed a new major concert work: *Serenade,* for violin, strings, and percussion, which had been commissioned by the Koussevitzky Foundation. This was a five-movement work based on Plato's *Symposium.* Each movement was devoted to one of five Greek philosophers or poets of the *Symposium* engaged in a discussion on love at the home of the poet, Agathon.

Bernstein himself conducted the world première of the

Serenade at the Venice Festival in Italy on September 12, 1954; Isaac Stern was the soloist. When the same conductor and soloist introduced this work in New York, at a concert of the Symphony of the Air, on April 18, 1956, Louis Biancolli wrote in the *World-Telegram:* "Mr. Bernstein's music moves adroitly from one movement to the next, each section growing naturally out of the previous one, and the whole building into a fabric of alternating energy and calm. . . . A reading of the dialogues inspired a fresh and pulsing score." In the *Herald Tribune,* Jay Harrison said that this composition "abounds in stretches of great beauty, and it frequently seems animated by a genuine poetic impulse. . . . The *Serenade* offers sufficient spice to attract and capture the ear."

Like the second symphony, *Serenade* was made into a ballet. Renamed *Serenade for Seven,* with choreography by Jerome Robbins, it received its world première in July 1959 at the Spoleto Festival in Italy, of which Gian-Carlo Menotti was founder and director. The ballet was introduced in the United States, in New York, in the spring of 1960.

CHAPTER 14

"The happy medium"

The same boundless energy and restless urge toward ever fuller and greater achievements that had made it impossible for Bernstein to confine himself to any single facet of music also refused to permit him to confine his efforts as a teacher of music. He conducted seminars during the regular semester at Brandeis University between 1951 and 1956, and during the summer he had his chores at Tanglewood. But this apparently was not enough. He started to seek out some other medium through which he could reach a still larger audience to infect with his own joy in music.

He found that medium in 1954 in television. Now the whole country was his classroom; now millions of music lovers were his students at a single session. Physically attractive, a man of outstanding charm, highly articulate, contagious in his enthusiasms, and endowed with a natural histrionic instinct, he could not fail to become one of televisions most popular personalities. "The man met the moment," as Abram Chasins said, "with his winning and photogenic personality, with his remarkable capacity to discuss all the aspects of the aural experience, to elucidate them in terms of both musicological and human experiences, and to illuminate them in dramatic interpretations."

The problem of analyzing great music to laymen had long intrigued him. He was impatient with what he has described as the "music appreciation racket," in which good music is explained to untrained listeners in terms of pretty stories, anecdotes, and extramusical interpretations often completely irrelevant to the music itself and incapable of conveying to the layman the essential esthetic purpose implicit in the sounds. He also knew that a strictly analytical approach for people unqualified to comprehend it would be a downright bore. But he was confident that "there is a happy medium somewhere between the music appreciation racket and purely technical discussion; it is hard to find, but it can be found." He found that medium by searching for and probing deeply into those very factors in a musical subject, or a musical composition, which made them so exciting to him personally. Then he would discuss his discoveries in simple, everyday English.

Bernstein made his first television appearance as music commentator on November 14, 1954, on the Omnibus Program. His topic was Beethoven's Fifth Symphony, specifically the first movement. This music, built as it was essentially from its four opening notes, represented something of a miracle to Bernstein. But this miracle did not lie in dramatic tales about Beethoven's deafness; nor in interpretations of these four notes as fate knocking at Beethoven's door; nor even in pointing up the fact that these notes had been used during World War II as a symbol of ultimate liberation and victory in nations subjugated by the Nazis. Numerous other analysts, commentators, annotators, and teachers have discussed Beethoven's Fifth Symphony in these or similar ways since time immemorial. But to Bernstein the wonder and awe of this music could not be conveyed to the listener by means of these explanations and interpretations. To Bernstein the music itself was the thing. In understanding the "struggle" of the composer to find the "right notes, right rhythms, right climaxes, right instrumentation" with which to follow his opening theme one could best come to an understanding of the music itself. This was the mystery of musical creation, of Beethoven's genius, and of the greatness of this composition.

To help him uncover this mystery, Bernstein went to Beethoven's notebooks, where the master had tussled with his basic ideas in his quest for the *mot juste*. As Bernstein explained in his broadcast: "The man rejected, rewrote, scratched out, tore up, and sometimes altered a passage as many as twenty times." Carefully and fastidiously, Bernstein led his audience through some of the many changes in harmony, tonality, and instrumentation to which Beethoven subjected his music before finally coming upon sounds that satisfied him. Bernstein showed his audience the way this music would have been if Beethoven had permitted his first ideas to remain unaltered. Then, by following the subtle and complex convolutions of Beethoven's musical thinking, Bernstein demonstrated how the music continually gained in the clarity of its logic, drama of its expression, power of its climaxes as Beethoven rewrote, refined, and recast his first ideas into a definitive version. Having shown how and why Beethoven wrote his music the way he did, Bernstein then proceeded to lead his orchestra in an uninterrupted performance of this movement.

This fresh and thoroughly musical approach to the problem of music appreciation was in a vocabulary anybody could understand. A similar method and approach has been brought to all other Bernstein's musical commentaries over television— and on an amazingly versatile range of subjects.

Under the incisive scalpel of his discerning analysis, he has been able to lay bare the heart, soul, and even the entrails of masterworks such as Beethoven's Ninth Symphony, Bach's *Magnificat,* Bach's *Passion According to St. Matthew,* and so forth. He pointed up the "almost atomic energy . . . its only equal in nature itself" in the opening movement of the Ninth Symphony. In discussing the *St. Matthew Passion* he revealed how Bach's musical world rested on the four corners of the chorale-prelude, the canon, and the fugue. Then he went on to demonstrate how through these strictly musical means Bach was able to underline the "suffering and pain," the "truth of redemption," the "drama," and the "religious spirit" of his text. "For Bach," Bernstein explained, "notes were not just sounds but the very stuff of creation. If he could use them to shape the Cross, or to depict a gesture of Christ's hand, or to suggest the flight of the spirit to heaven, then he was happy."

In his talk on Mozart he revealed that a mighty genius was able to conform to the musical clichés of his age and yet translate these clichés into overwhelming emotional experiences. A discourse on modern music clarified why these works sounded the way they did in readily comprehensible images and metaphors. He used an analogue from baseball to explain tonality; showed what dissonance was by playing on the piano "America" with one hand and "The Star-Spangled Banner" with the other; described cross rhythms in terms of a George Gershwin tune, "Fidgety Feet." He has compared a Bach fugue to an Erector Set and Ravel's *Bolero* to a "high-class hootchy-kootchy dance."

What makes opera grand, what is the job of the conductor, what makes music humorous, what is jazz, how has American musical comedy evolved, what has rhythm contributed to great music, what has been the role of musical instruments from ancient recorders and sackbuts to present-day curiosities like the kazoo and the tape recorder—these and similar subjects carried to millions of new music lovers an altogether new concept of a great and formerly bewildering art.

"His talks," said Howard Taubman, "set an unsurpassed standard of musical literacy on the airwaves; they exuded charm and showmanship; they showed that Mr. Bernstein, a protean figure as conductor, pianist, and composer, could use the home screen to communicate the wonder of music to millions across the country in a virtuoso teaching performance." For these millions—many of whom had never taken a lesson

116

in music and thus could neither read nor play a note—Bernstein had succeeded in making the sound of music a stirring adventure and an unforgettable experience.

Bernstein had also achieved a happy medium between his private and social life and his musical and professional one.

On September 8, 1952, a daughter, Jamie, was born to Lenny and Felicia. A son, Alexander Serge (named after Koussevitzky), arrived on July 7, 1955. The Bernstein family now occupied a nine-room duplex apartment on 57th Street, catercorner to Carnegie Hall. There their needs were attended to by a staff that included a Chilean nursemaid for the children, a Chilean cook, and Bernstein's personal secretary, Helen Coates.

Bernstein has remarked lightly that eight of these nine rooms belong to his family, while only one—baptized his "thinking room"—is his. Since he prefers keeping the windows covered by lowered Venetian blinds, and since the color of the walls and the carpet is a drab gray, this working room at first sight seems unusually somber. And unusually crowded. Bernstein's scores, sheet music, books, recordings, volumes upon volumes of scrapbooks of clippings, are all piled in huge bookcases. A portable phonograph, a recording apparatus, his papers and pencils, and two telephones clutter the enormous table on which he does his writing. Nearby is a couch on which he often sprawls while studying scores, or working out some pressing musical problem, or while just thinking. Nearby, too, is his grand piano. (Two smaller pianos stand back to back in the living room.)

Bernstein comes to this studio early each day, frequently at dawn. He prepares for himself a cup of coffee on a hot plate, then picks up one of the scores he is conducting that week for a two-hour period of intensive study. A more generous breakfast is partaken at about 8:30 that morning, usually with one or more people with whom he must discuss some business. When breakfast is over, he returns to study. Shortly after 9:30 he leaves his "thinking room" and crosses the street to Carnegie Hall for the day's rehearsal with his orchestra. After the rehearsal, his day's work really begins. He must now attend to numerous conferences with agents, managers, producers; meet newspapermen for interviews; discuss various projects with collaborators; make copious notes on some piece of music he is working on at the moment; plan his lectures. When friends come to his apartment for dinner he will often join them in playing anagrams or discussing books, plays, or politics. Somewhere along the line he finds the time to play with his children, or to join his wife in informal performances of two-piano music.

On the evenings of his concerts, he eats sparingly, and reaches the hall well in advance of concert time. During the intermission his wife massages him with cologne. (There are times, before the concert, when she even cuts his hair.) While the massaging is going on, he usually grumbles about the things that went wrong with his performance or, if all went well, of places where an improvement could still be made. The concert ended, he meets swarms of friends, colleagues, and acquaintances in the artist's room. Then he partakes of an expansive meal and usually goes off with his wife to some social function.

Just as he has departmentalized his mind to perform several jobs simultaneously, so he has systematized his day to find enough time for everything that must be done. Whenever he finds a free moment—on a train, in a taxi, at an airport, in hotel lobbies—he also finds the capacity of plunging into work completely oblivious of his surroundings or distractions. His powers of concentration are enormous, and with them he possesses an indefatigable vitality. As his wife once said: "Lenny never does anything in moderation. If we're playing anagrams, he always wants to play till dawn. If we watch the 'Late Show' on TV he always wants to watch the 'Late Late

Show' after that. If we go to a movie, he will want to step into another movie right away. If he plays with the children, he plays long and hard."

Bernstein has said that "it's perfectly possible to do all the things I have to." This is true, mainly because there is simply no musical problem he cannot solve easily and effortlessly. There just is nothing he cannot do in music, whether it is to learn a monumental score in a short period of time, play a technically demanding concerto on the piano with almost no preliminary practice, write a huge symphony, dash off a pop tune, or arrive at some fresh, new viewpoints for his television commentaries.

Despite all his facility, and all his successes, he is really a perpetual worrier—in continual torment that what he has just done was not good enough or that what he is about to do won't come off as well as he hopes. He (who is always being praised so extravagantly) frets when the critics make some disparaging remark about him. He abhors hearing people call him "versatile" or telling him he is trying to do too many things. He is put out by the fact that he has never really written an outstandingly successful hit tune. And, strange as it may sound of a man who has already achieved the highest pinnacles of fame, he worries most of all about his artistic future.

CHAPTER 15

"Who do I think I am— everybody?"

Bernstein's first and only box-office failure on Broadway came in 1956 with *Candide*. *Candide* is the 18th-century satire by Voltaire mocking the optimism of a school of philosophers headed by Leibnitz. Lillian Hellman made the adaptation for the musical stage; and the lyrics for Bernstein's songs were provided by Dorothy Parker, John La Touche, and Richard Wilbur.

In the musical play, as in the Voltaire novel, Candide is a confirmed optimist, having been taught by his mentor, Dr. Pangloss, that this is the best of all possible worlds. Accompanied by his sweetheart, Cunegonde, Candide decides to leave his home in Westphalia in search of truth, goodness, and honesty. As they wander from one city to another—Lisbon, Paris, Buenos Aires, and so on—they confront only tragedy and disaster, misery and human greed. At one place Candide is beaten, and at another he is cheated. He is even dragged down helplessly to the low moral level of the world around him. Bitter and disillusioned, he decides to settle down at last to cultivate his own garden. He marries Cunegonde, who by now is old and ugly.

Lillian Hellman's adaptation was bold and incisive, rich with

Leonard Bernstein
conducts
The New York Philharmonic

Voltaire's mockery and malice. The best lyrics had the sting of sharp rapier thrusts. Robert Coleman said in the *Mirror* that *Candide* "towers head and shoulders above most of the song-and-dancers you'll get this or any other season. It has wry humor, mannered grace, and marvelous music."

The "marvelous music" was truly a cornucopia of riches. Beginning with a sprightly overture which has *opéra-bouffe* sparkle and vivacity (Bernstein has included it occasionally at some of his symphony concerts), the score went on to include such gay and tender melodies as "Eldorado" and "What's the Use?" and such witty and effervescent tunes as "Glitter and Be Gay" and "The Best of All Possible Worlds." In addition, the score contained parodies of opera arias, folk songs, music-hall ditties; trios, quartets, choral numbers; a waltz, mazurka, ballad, tango, gavotte. "None of his previous theater music," wrote Brooks Atkinson, "has the joyous variety, humor, and richness of this score."

For all its attractions—and these were truly many and varied —*Candide* failed to attract audiences into the Martin Beck Theater. It opened on December 1, 1956 and was forced to close after only 73 performances. It may well have been, as some said, that its title was a deficit; that a sprightlier and more commercial name might have convinced audiences that this was not merely an adaptation of a classic but an evening overflowing with entertainment and merriment. Or Brooks Atkinson may have been right when he maintained that "the eighteenth-century philosophical tale is not ideal material for a theater show." In any event, *Candide* came and went—but it was much better than its brief day would suggest.

However, it did not pass into complete obscurity after the final curtain in New York. In 1958–1959 a concert version toured the United States. And on April 30, 1959, it was given in London at the Saville Theater. "I hail this as the strongest, wittiest musical score in town," reported John Thompson in the *Daily Express*. "This is an evening of high style. I feel sure Americans were wrong."

As far as Bernstein himself was concerned, he was much too busy to feel anything more than passing regret or disappointment at the failure of *Candide*. Even while this show was breathing its last heavy gasps in January of 1957, he was occupied with many different tasks. He was conducting the New York Philharmonic, knee-deep at work on a new Broadway musical show, and writing a script on modern music for one of the Omnibus programs on TV. Such whirlwind activity gained ever greater momentum as the year of 1957 progressed. Beyond his many appearances with orchestras everywhere, he had a new script to write (this time on Bach) for a March appearance on television. During the summer he had his teaching duties at Tanglewood, as well as performances with the Boston Symphony. After that he had to make some recordings for Columbia. And all the while he was putting the finishing touches on his new Broadway musical, participating in the casting problems, and assisting at rehearsals. Then, one day after his Broadway musical opened, he flew to Israel to conduct the Israel Philharmonic for the opening of the new Frederick R. Mann Auditorium. No sooner had he returned to America, a month later, than he had to memorize both the piano and the orchestral parts of Shostakovich's new Second Piano Concerto for one of the concerts of the New York Philharmonic. He also had to prepare the programs for six weeks of performances with the same orchestra, and write about half a dozen new scripts for his various talks both over television and in Carnegie Hall.

The humor, even absurdity, of such frenetic activity did not fail to strike him. At one moment he stopped short and asked himself in bewilderment: "Who do I think I am—*everybody?*"

The musical production engaging Bernstein in 1957 was *West Side Story*. It opened at the Winter Garden on September 26 of that year. Its run there of 734 performances represented the greatest box-office (as well as artistic) triumph Bernstein had thus far encountered in the theater. Then, after an extended nationwide tour, *West Side Story* returned to the Winter Garden to begin a new engagement in April 1960.

The original idea for *West Side Story* came from Jerome Robbins, who then interested Arthur Laurents in writing the text, and Bernstein the music. Robbins' initial idea—a modern version of Shakespeare's *Romeo and Juliet*—placed two adolescents separated by religious differences against the setting of New York's Lower East Side. At that time—in 1949—the project remained little more than a conversation piece, since all three men had more pressing contractual commitments. But a few years later, when they met at a party, they discussed the problem of juvenile delinquency, then so alive in the news. "There it was," recalls Arthur Laurents. "Time had brought us a new, a better background for the musical: today's confused adolescents forming gangs to give them a sense of belonging to *something,* two juvenile gangs for 'both your houses'! Excitement turned into plans, promises, cross-my-heart-hope-to-die pledges."

Early in 1954, both Laurents and Bernstein were in Hollywood. Bernstein was then at work on the "brittle, brilliant and brutal" background music for the motion picture starring Marlon Brando, *Waterfront* (his score subsequently was nominated for but did not win the Academy Award). While sunning themselves at the pool of the Beverly Hills Hotel, Laurents and Bernstein started once again to discuss their ideas for their long-neglected musical. "We had begun with religion," says Laurents, "but that was dropped into the roomy swimming pool. Instead, the racial problems of Los Angeles influenced us to shift our play from the Lower East Side of New York to the Upper West Side, and the conflict to that between a Puerto Rican gang and a polymorphous self-styled 'American gang.' "

When Bernstein was back in New York the story and the background of his musical jelled further in his mind one day while he was driving his car. Taking a wrong exit on the Henry Hudson Parkway he came into the heart of New York's Portuguese section. "Somehow," he later recalled, "I was under a huge causeway, somewhere right by the river up around 125th Street. All around Puerto Rican kids were playing—with the causeway as a background in a classic key, pillars, and Roman arches. The contrast between the setting and the kids was striking, fascinating. Right then and there we had our theme for *West Side Story*—a contemporary setting echoing a classic myth. Right then and there I even had the inspiration for the 'Rumble' scene."

And so, Shakespeare's Verona became the crowded slums of Manhattan; Romeo and Juliet were transformed into Tony and Maria, the latter a Portuguese girl; the famous balcony scene from Shakespeare's tragedy became an idyl on a fire escape; the feud of the Capulets and the Montagues was changed into a life-and-death rivalry between two teen-age gangs. One of these gangs was the Jets, to which Tony belonged and which dedicated itself to the proposition that no Puerto Ricans must be permitted to penetrate the Jets' territory. The other gang, named the Sharks, was made up entirely of Puerto Ricans, its leader being Maria's brother. Tony and Maria first meet in a gymnasium dance where they fall in love. Since they are of rival factions they must, from this point on, carry on their romance in secrecy. They eventually go through a kind of mock marriage ceremony in a bridal shop where Maria is employed, the dress dummies serving as their only guests. When a gang war erupts between the two factions, Tony kills Maria's brother;

then he, in turn, meets retribution through murder by one of the Sharks.

This kind of dramatic material, compelling in its realism and provocative with social problems, is perhaps more suitable for the operatic stage than for the popular theater. And the musical play that finally emerged from the pens of Jerome Robbins, Arthur Laurents, Bernstein, and the lyricist Stephen Sondheim, had operatic dimensions. For one thing, dance was emphasized to a point where it was required to carry on much of the dramatic action, and in a way never before attempted on Broadway. *West Side Story* opens with a sinister dance performed by the two rival gangs against the somber background of a gaunt warehouse. The play achieves a climatic point with an exciting mambo in a gymnasium. In "Somewhere," a dream sequence, the romantic overtones of the play are gently sounded, while in "The Rumble" the grim and savage mood of gang war is discussed in dance movements.

The ugliness, the bitterness, the agony, and the neuroticism of slum life in the city streets could also be found in Bernstein's music; these, and fleeting moments of poetry and beauty and hope that sometimes touch the lives of these tortured adolescents. The overture is nervous, discordant, high-tensioned; so are many of the musical episodes utilized as background tone-painting for some of the stage action, and some of the music for the dance episodes. The songs "Maria," "I Feel Pretty," "Somewhere," and "Tonight" provide a tender contrast to satirical ditties like "America" and "Gee, Officer Krupke." "Mr. Bernstein," wrote John McClain in the *Journal-American,* "is responsible for the true importance of the piece, for the music is always magnificent. There are passages worthy of grand opera, there are almost numbers which would do credit to a 'pop' musical, and the incidental phrases which highlight the scenes are memorable."

In discussing *West Side Story,* Brooks Atkinson said: "The

125

subject is not beautiful. But what *West Side Story* draws out of it is beautiful. For it has a searching point of view. . . . Everything . . . is of a piece. Everything contributes to the total impression of wildness, ecstasy, and anguish." Equally enthusiastic responses came from the other critics. "The show rides with a catastrophic roar," remarked Walter Kerr in the *Herald Tribune*. Robert Coleman called it "sensational. . . . It has earthy humor and simple beauty and, best of all, it has tremendous drive. It moves with the speed of a switchblade knife thrust." Frank Aston in the *World-Telegram* said: "By the magic of good music and artistic movement it built up moments of theatrical beauty."

Such unqualified enthusiasm was not restricted to the United States alone. On December 12, 1958, when *West Side Story* opened at Her Majesty's Theater in London, it received an acclaim equaled by few other American musicals. As one reporter cabled to *Variety:* "There was not a word of criticism in the reviews which appeared in the dailies the following morning, and at least one notice suggested that the new arrival topped *My Fair Lady*." Characteristic of the English reaction to *West Side Story* were the following comments: "It is a most dynamic, vital, and electric musical show" (Harold Conway in the *Daily Sketch*); "this great musical show begins a new age in the theater" (John Thompson in the *Daily Express*); "it struck London like a flash of lightning set to music, the most dynamic, dramatic, operatic, balletic and acrobatic of all these epics from Broadway" (Cecil Wilson in the *Daily Mail*).

At long last, Leonard Bernstein had a symphony orchestra of his own: Early in 1957, Dimitri Mitropoulos, music director of the New York Philharmonic, announced that Bernstein had been engaged to share with him the direction of that orchestra for the coming 1957–1958 season. With eloquent appropriateness, the man who had first recognized Bernstein's

126

potential as a conductor, and who had also been the first to convince him to consider conducting as a career, was the man who was now offering him one of the most desirable musical posts in the world. "I am sure," said Mitropoulos in commenting further on the Bernstein appointment, "that together we will be able to prepare a very sound and stimulating season."

But the new 1957–1958 season hardly had an opportunity to pick up steam and hit full stride when an even more dramatic announcement took place. On November 19, at a luncheon at the Century Club in New York tendered by David M. Keiser, president of the New York Philharmonic, Mitropoulos announced that at the termination of that season he was completely relinquishing his permanent association with the orchestra. On the heels of this announcement came another that, on Mitropoulos' suggestion and with the full approval of the directors of the New York Philharmonic, Leonard Bernstein had been engaged as the orchestra's new music director. He was one of the youngest men, and the only one of American birth, ever to hold this office. In accepting this honor, Bernstein did not fail to recall the part Mitropoulos had played in his own career. "Twenty-one years later to hear him abdicate is at once heartbreaking for me and at the same time it fills me with a sense of responsibility." Nor did Bernstein neglect to remark that his assumption of the post of music director had for him a gratifying "sense of rightness, of naturalness." The New York Philharmonic, after all, had been the first symphony orchestra he had ever conducted; it had also been the first symphony orchestra to give him a job.

The first New York Philharmonic concert led by Bernstein following this public announcement came on January 2, 1958. It provided him with an opportunity to cast a nostalgic, sentimental glance at the past. Two of the numbers he performed that day had also appeared on the program with which he made his debut fourteen years earlier: the *Manfred Overture* by Schumann and Richard Strauss' *Don Quixote*. "His way with them revealed how far he had matured without losing his gusto and flair for the dramatic," reported Howard Taubman. But almost as if to emphasize further that he did not live entirely in the past, this program was also the one on which Bernstein played and conducted the American première of Shostakovich's Second Piano Concerto.

ENTR'ACTE II

"The History of the Philharmonic Is the History of Music in America"

Thus Leonard Bernstein has become the latest in the magistral line of great conductors to become permanently associated with the New York Philharmonic Orchestra.

The New York Philharmonic is the oldest functioning symphony orchestra in America. Already more than a half century ago its musical significance was acknowledged when the eminent New York critic, James Gibbons Huneker, wrote that "the history of the Philharmonic is the history of music in America." The orchestra came into being more than a century ago—in April 1842. At that time a group of dedicated New York music lovers gathered at the Apollo Rooms at 410 Broadway to draw up plans for the creation of a symphony orchestra. When later the same year the first rehearsals took place, the owner of the Apollo Rooms had so little faith in the survival of the quixotic undertaking that he demanded his rental fee paid in advance before each rehearsal. Consequently, as the men of the orchestra filed into the auditorium, each one contributed twenty-five cents toward the rent.

The first concert took place at the Apollo Rooms on December 7, 1842. Three conductors participated in that program. U. C.

129

Hill led a performance of Beethoven's Fifth Symphony; H. C. Timm, an overture by Johann Wenzel Kalliwoda; and D. Etienne the *Oberon Overture* of Karl Maria von Weber.

During the first decade of its existence, the Philharmonic was directed at each of its concerts sometimes by two, and sometimes by three conductors. Members of the orchestra owning dress clothes were required to wear them at the public performance; all others were allowed to wear dark trousers and frock coat. As an economy measure, some of the orchestra players were required to serve as ushers before the concert. Another untraditional practice was to have the orchestra men perform standing, with the exception of the cellists.

For many seasons, the orchestra gave only four concerts a year. The musicians were paid on a co-operative basis. By the end of the 15th season, the men were able to divide a kitty of $4,810 and thus earn $143 each for a season's labor. In the 16th season, the number of concerts a year was increased to five; in 1869, to six.

Meanwhile, in 1865, the orchestra finally acquired a single permanent conductor in whom full authority was vested. He was Carl Bergmann, who for some time before this had been sharing the dais with Theodore Eisfeld. Bergmann remained the permanent conductor of the Philharmonic for twenty-one years. An uncompromising champion of the then new music of Wagner and Liszt, Bergmann was not popular with his audiences. More than once during his long tenure it seemed that the orchestra was about to perish from lack of box-office nourishment. Artistically as well as financially, there were serious problems for the orchestra. Because the musicians were unable to earn a living wage exclusively from these concerts, they had to take on other, profitable assignments. The result was that on many occasions the musicians were required by their other commitments to send substitutes for some of the rehearsals, and occasionally even for the concerts themselves. It was a rare occa-

130

sion, indeed, when Bergmann could perform a concert with all the men he had previously rehearsed. Sometimes when a solo clarinet player or a solo bassoon player failed to show up for the performance, those parts had to be hurriedly assigned to a violin or cello respectively. As late as 1900 this strange situation continued to harass Philharmonic conductors. Walter Damrosch wrote in his autobiography of his own experiences in those years: "I found to my amazement that of the hundred players at the concert less than fifty were actual members of that organization. . . . Most of the wind instruments were outsiders and therefore could not be properly controlled regarding attendance or rehearsals."

Bergmann left the Philharmonic in 1876 and was succeeded by Dr. Leopold Damrosch, the father of Walter. That season rep-represented the lowest ebb in the tide of the orchestra's history. Total receipts for the season reached a niggardly $841, hardly enough to pay the men anything for their work that year. Once again it appeared that the orchestra was about to gasp its last breath.

In 1877 a new conductor was found for the orchestra— Theodore Thomas. It was his popularity that helped give the orchestra a new lease on life. In his fourteen-year period as permanent conductor, Thomas succeeded in increasing the attendance at his concerts to a point where in his last season the income from the six concerts reached the respectable figure of $15,000.

After the turn of the 20th century, an expansion program was instituted for the Philharmonic, in which the number of concerts per season was augmented to eight, each led by some outstanding visitor from Europe. Some of Europe's most brilliant conductors now crossed the Atlantic to direct the Philharmonic, among them being Richard Strauss, Felix Weingartner, Edouard Colonne, and Vassily Safonov.

In 1907 an important milestone was reached by the orchestra.

131

A radical reorganization took place in which the orchestra was established for the first time on a more or less sound financial basis. A sixteen-week season was instituted with Vassily Safonov as permanent conductor. Two years after that Gustav Mahler took over the baton. His four-year regime was a glowing chapter in American music, for it was with Mahler that the New York Philharmonic became one of America's most renowned musical organizations.

After Mahler came Josef Stransky, who held the post of principal conductor for a dozen years. One year after Stransky's appointment, Joseph Pulitzer endowed the orchestra with a million dollars to allow for further reforms. Not only was the season expanded again, this time to twenty-three weeks, but also a daily rehearsal schedule was formulated. During this Stransky era, the personnel of the orchestra was strengthened through a merger with the National Symphony in 1921. A second important amalgamation took place in 1928 when the New York Philharmonic absorbed the New York Symphony Society, which for many years had been directed by Walter Damrosch.

Two world famous musicians now helped bring the New York Philharmonic to the very front rank of the world's symphonic organizations. One was Willem Mengelberg, conductor of the renowned Concertgebouw Orchestra of Amsterdam, Holland. Mengelberg maintained a permanent association with the Philharmonic from 1922 to 1930. The other was Arturo Toscanini who, after a sensational Philharmonic debut in 1928, was its permanent conductor from 1930 to 1936. John Barbirolli succeeded Toscanini and stayed until 1943. After him came Artur Rodzinski, and in 1950 Dimitri Mitropoulos, from whom Bernstein inherited his post.

PART THREE

*"And All the Clouds That Lour'd upon
Our House in the Deep Bosom of the
Ocean Buried."*

CHAPTER 16

"What an orchestra!—
I am a happy man"

The all-consuming demands now made on him by
the New York Philharmonic finally compelled Bernstein to
concentrate his fullest energies on conducting. From mid-Oc-
tober to April, each season, the New York Philharmonic gives
over a hundred concerts. To plan the orchestra's over-all artistic
program is a task of formidable proportions. Guest conductors
and artists must be selected; the entire season's repertory must
be carefully planned to combine the familiar with the new. To
add still further to Bernstein's burden was the fact that he himself was required to conduct some forty of these concerts. In
the past—as a guest conductor of many different orchestras in
many different places—he could repeat works with which he
was thoroughly familiar. But as the principal conductor of a

133

single orchestra he had to refurbish his repertory continually to keep his concerts alive and vital with premières and novelties. The amount of new music he now had to study and learn each week was prodigious.

Then there were peripheral duties. He had to prepare material for his discussions on music—not only for the increasing number of television programs he was now required to assume, but also for the Saturday morning concerts for young people which he insisted on undertaking. There were recordings to be made all the time for Columbia. And there were the extended postseason tours with his orchestra.

"The Philharmonic is it," he told an interviewer when he assumed the post of music director. "This is my full-time job. I'm going to give it everything I have. And if I fail, I fail honestly." Henceforth he reduced to a bare minimum the number of his guest appearances with other orchestras. For a long time, he wrote no music whatsoever, serious or popular. And while it was true that his commitments for television and records were now augmented, all this was done in collaboration with his orchestra and consequently fell within the framework of the orchestra's activities each season. Only one of his former demanding connections was maintained, his summer program of teaching and conducting at Tanglewood, but even from here he was soon required to take a leave-of-absence.

His new job with the Philharmonic might have been greatly simplified if he were willing to follow familiar grooves in the planning and the presentation of his concerts. But he had no intention of pursuing a traditional course. From the moment he became music director he was driven by the compulsion to undertake the new, the untried, the unorthodox.

For one thing, he insisted that the over-all program each season conform more or less to some consistent plan or follow some integrating motive. As he said, "An orchestra like the Philharmonic has to be different from that of other orchestras because it is New York, the center of the musical world. The programs should add up to something; they should have a theme running through them. There should always be a sense of festival about going to the Philharmonic." In line with such thinking he initiated a survey of American music from such older personalities as MacDowell, Ives, Foote, and Gilbert to such young and comparatively unknown figures as Easley Blackwood and Kenneth Gaburo. He introduced cycles of concerts devoted to the concerto; to Mahler in honor of the composer's centenary; to Pergolesi for his 250th birthday; to Handel commemorating that master's bicentenary; to music for the theater; to 20th-century problems in music.

He had other innovations. When he first became director he tried having his men wear a special outfit for rehearsals. This practice was subjected by the players to such ridicule and attack that it had to be abandoned. But other experiments were far more fruitful. And one of the most significant of these was the "Preview Concerts" initiated in the 1958–1959 season. Bernstein had long felt it would be advantageous for him and his orchestra to have the last rehearsal played before a live audience, as was sometimes the practice in Europe. Once this idea began to crystallize in his mind, he decided to extend it to permit that final rehearsal to become a kind of forum in which he could discuss with his audiences various musical subjects in general, but specifically the composers and the music he was performing that evening.

He revamped the Philharmonic schedule to make the Thursday evening series the "Preview Concerts"—performances in which the formal concert of the following afternoon was supplemented by informal comments by the conductor.

The first "Preview" took place on the opening night of the 1958–1959 season, on October 1. The formal program included William Schuman's *American Festival Overture,* Charles Ives' Second Symphony, and Beethoven's Seventh Symphony. There

135

was also a "surprise," Berlioz' *Roman Carnival Overture* played as an encore. Between these numbers Bernstein talked, sang, and played the piano. All the while he maintained an informal manner by criticizing his own singing and piano playing. He spoke about the strange, unique personality of Ives, who had been an insurance man most of his life and who preferred leading a lonely, isolated existence in Connecticut while writing his music and allowing it to gather dust on the shelves. He explained why Ives wrote the kind of experimental music he did.

"If his maiden effort at a 'preview' was any measure of what is to come," wrote Howard Taubman, "audiences are going to have a lot of fun. Occasionally they may be irritated, but they rarely will be bored."

The "Preview" became an immediate, outstanding hit with the public. It soon became impossible to beg, steal, borrow, or buy a ticket for a Thursday evening concert. The following season subscriptions for this series jumped more than 75 per cent over the previous year; by the time that season began the series had been subscribed 99 per cent.

The impact of Bernstein's cogent, colorful, and charming personality was felt in all the other Philharmonic series as well. Attendance jumped 20 per cent in his second season as music director. For the first time in the history of the orchestra, advance sale for tickets for the 1959–1960 season passed the million-dollar mark. Such was the appeal of Bernstein's concerts that twenty additional ones had to be added to the regular schedule. It was also due to Bernstein's personal magnetism and popularity that the radio network of CBS, which broadcast the Philharmonic concerts over its nationwide network on Saturday evenings, had to add seventy more stations to its hookup, bringing the total to well over two hundred. Bernstein was also the reason why the Philharmonic for the first time was being sponsored for television performances, by the Lincoln

Division of the Ford Motor Company and in 1960–1961 by Ford Motor Company and Shell Oil; why the recording program had to be amplified as the sale of Bernstein's records soared; why extensive tours out of New York had to be continually projected for the orchestra.

There could, then, be little question but that Bernstein had the natural gift for creating rapport between himself and his public. But if, as many critics remarked, the Philharmonic seemed to acquire a "new sound" under Bernstein—an enthusiasm, feeling of excitement, electricity, and cohesion in its playing it had not known for some years—it was also because Bernstein had a rare gift of capturing the affection, co-operation, and enthusiasm of the men who worked under him.

The men of the orchestra were, of course, grateful to him because his fabulous popularity made possible for them heavy increases in revenue each year. But there were other reasons, too, why they worked so enthusiastically for him. They liked the way—despite his awesome office of music director—he never tried to put on a false pose of grandeur; the way he never assumed dictatorial attitudes; the way he never badgered them. If one of them made a mistake at a rehearsal, he would often disregard it discreetly; then when the passage was repeated and the mistake was rectified, he would smile pleasantly at the perpetrator. He himself might suffer inner torment when something went wrong at a concert, but he rarely inflicted his own personal suffering on the ones to blame. He would merely talk gently to the offender and explain how such mistakes could best be avoided in the future.

The orchestra liked his lively manner, his informal ways, his charm and gaiety both at and away from rehearsals. The men appreciated the fact that he always stood ready to praise them when they played well. "What an orchestra!" he once exclaimed after a rehearsal. "What sensitivity! What vigor! I'm a happy man!"

One of the men of the orchestra reflected not merely his own personal reaction but that of his colleagues when he remarked to this writer: "We worshiped Toscanini, but we love Lenny." Love from men he must necessarily drive long and hard in order to attain the best possible performance is perhaps the most eloquent tribute an orchestra can pay its conductor.

CHAPTER 17

"Audiences are the same the world over"

On April 27, 1958, Leonard Bernstein and the New York Philharmonic embarked on two planes for a tour of South and Central America. (Two additional planes carried eight tons of baggage and the instruments.) The sponsorship was President Eisenhower's Special International Program for Cultural Presentations administered by the American National Theater and Academy. During the next 7 weeks, they traveled 15,000 miles, gave 39 concerts in 21 cities of 12 different countries. The paying audience totaled more than 200,000 but a far greater audience heard some of these concerts over radio and television. During the first 4½ weeks Bernstein was the orchestra's sole conductor. Sometimes he led as many as 6 performances a week, occasionally filling the role of pianist-conductor in performances of the Ravel G major Concerto. Dimitri Mitropoulos later conducted 11 concerts. For Mitropoulos these were to be his first appearances in South America; Bernstein's only previous performances there had been in 1954, in Brazil.

The tour's opening concert took place in Panama City; the closing one, in Mexico City. Between these two widely separated geographical points the orchestra was heard in Caracas and Maracaibo in Venezuela; Bogotá in Colombia; La Paz in Bolivia; Asunción in Paraguay; Santiago and Viña del Mar in

Chile; Buenos Aires, Mendoza, and Córdoba in Argentina; Quito in Ecuador; Montevideo in Uruguay; and São Paulo, Rio de Janeiro, and Porto Alegre in Brazil. Never before had a major symphony orchestra undertaken such an extensive jaunt through the South and Central American countries. Some of the cities visited had never before heard an orchestra of international importance; in others, their only contact with symphonic music had been through performances by a local ensemble. It is then easy to see why the New York Philharmonic under Bernstein should have been a revelation to music lovers there.

On each of his programs, Bernstein played at least one contemporary American work by Copland, Roy Harris, Barber, Gershwin, Schuman, and Charles Turner. Each concert was also prefaced by the playing of the American national anthem and that of the visited country. In Venezuela, the President implored Bernstein to repeat his performance of the Venezulean anthem because he had never before heard it played so beautifully.

Wherever they came, orchestra and conductor were given a hero's welcome: feted by local officials and music groups, by American embassies and cultural organizations. At the concerts there were always unparalleled demonstrations of enthusiasm. It was impossible to meet the demand for tickets. Box-office records were smashed in one city after another. In São Paulo there was such a storm of protest on the part of those unable to gain admission into the Municipal Theater for the three scheduled concerts that a special performance was hastily improvised in an open-air auditorium accommodating thirty thousand. There was almost a riot threatening to tear apart the theater in La Paz, instigated by those who could not buy a ticket. At the Bolivar Theater in Quito seats had to be improvised wherever there was an empty space. When, in Montevideo, the day on which the box office would open for the sale of tickets was announced, thousands queued up outside the theater twenty-four hours before the sale began; these music lovers, equipped with food and mattresses, waited patiently through the night for the box office to open.

Nobody, it seemed, would stay away if he could help it. Heads of states down to the humblest swarmed to the auditoriums. The Presidents of Ecuador, Brazil, Peru, and Paraguay received Bernstein in their official boxes during intermission to express their enthusiasm. In La Paz, the President attended the city's opening concert even though only a few hours earlier he had put down a revolt in the provinces. In Bogotá, General Gabriel Paris made an appearance, though only two days before this he had been kidnapped and wounded in a police rebellion. In Quito and Córdoba, local professional musicians stood three-deep in the wings of the stage listening to the concerts.

In Quito, Ecuador, Bernstein and some of the Philharmonic men were so affected by the altitude that midway in the program they were forced to take deep breaths of oxygen. Nevertheless the quality of the performance was not affected. "Never has Quito enjoyed such superb music," exclaimed Ernest Xanco, director of the Quito National Orchestra. He was speaking for himself, but he might well have been speaking for all of South and Central America.

Ambitious and unprecedented though this tour had been, it was only the prelude for a greater, more historic, more precedent-shattering jaunt the following year. The fervent, passionate Latin-American reactions to Leonard Bernstein's musicmaking were hardly more than echoes when compared to the storms of approval aroused in 1959 when the New York Philharmonic under Bernstein made an epoch-making tour of Europe, the Near East, and countries behind the Iron Curtain. Once again these concerts were made possible by President Eisenhower's Special International Program for Cultural Presentations.

This musical voyage began in Athens, Greece, on August 5,

1959. During the next 10 weeks, the orchestra gave 50 concerts in 29 cities of 17 countries: Athens and Salonika in Greece; Baalbek in Lebanon; Istanbul in Turkey; Salzburg in Austria; Warsaw in Poland; Moscow, Leningrad, and Kiev in the Soviet Union; Scheveningen in Holland; Düsseldorf, Essen, Wiesebaden, Munich, Hamburg, and Berlin in Germany; Luxembourg; Paris in France; Basel in Switzerland; Belgrade and Zagreb in Yugoslavia; Venice and Milan in Italy; Oslo in Norway; Helsinki and Turku in Finland; Stockholm and Göteborg in Sweden; and London in England. Five festivals were included, those at Athens, Baalbek, Salzburg, Venice, and Berlin; at Baalbek and Salzburg this was the first time an American orchestra was represented. In Moscow, the concerts were given in conjunction with the American Exposition opened there that summer by Vice President Nixon.

Bernstein conducted thirty-seven of these concerts, the others being directed by two other young Americans, Thomas Schippers and Seymour Lipkin. The repertory embraced classic symphonies, concertos, and other familiar repertory works; but with them came modern American music by Barber, Bernstein (*The Age of Anxiety*), Copland, Diamond, Gershwin, Ives, and Piston. In three compositions Bernstein appeared both as pianist and conductor: Gershwin's *Rhapsody in Blue,* Beethoven's Triple Concerto, and Mozart's Piano Concerto in G major, K. 453.

This was the most extensive tour ever undertaken by the New York Philharmonic, as well as the most triumphant. This was also the first time this orchestra performed in the Soviet Union and other Iron Curtain countries; the first time that any American orchestra appeared abroad conducted exclusively by native-born musicians.

So much for essential facts and details.

As the journey progressed from one city to the next, from one country to another, dramatic incident piled upon dramatic incident, ovation followed ovation, in tidal waves. After the Warsaw concert, there took place a forty-five minute demonstration. The ovation in Munich was arrested only after Bernstein and the orchestra played two encores. In Oslo, the concert proved the most significant musical event in that city in many years; it was attended by King Olav V, Princess Astrid, and Ambassadors from most of the major European countries as well as that of the United States. In Yugoslavia, one critic said of the orchestra, "I never heard sound like that before," while a second critic called it "the best orchestra I have ever heard." At The Hague, the critic of *Het Vaderland* described the performance as "phenomenal." In Basel, Dr. Fritz Ernst (music critic for the local newspaper, and director of the Basel Radio) said, in commenting on the audience reaction: "We have never seen anything like this before."

Music lovers stood patiently outside the concert hall—often for hours outside the hotel where Bernstein and the orchestra were stopping—to have a look at the musicians, touch them, shout their affection and admiration. And so it went, ever more rapturous praises from the critics, ever more hysterical responses from audiences, ever more sentimental tokens of esteem and affection and simple homage from the masses.

But it was the Soviet Union that proved for Bernstein the most overwhelming experience of the tour, and probably of his entire career.

The first concert in the Soviet Union took place at the concert hall of the Tschaikovsky Conservatory in Moscow on August 22. The enthusiasm of the audience began to percolate with Bernstein's stirring presentation of the Soviet national anthem with which the concert opened (played in a brisker tempo than that to which Russians are accustomed). After that, the excitement kept mounting spiral-like from one number to the next, from Barber's *Essay No. 2* through Mozart's Piano Concerto in G major, the latter providing Soviet music lovers with what for them was an unfamiliar spectacle of having a musician double as conductor and solo pianist. The culmination of the excitement that night was reached after a breathless performance of the Shostakovich Fifth Symphony. An official of the Tschaikovsky Conservatory later said: "This is the first time we have heard Shostakovich played so well." Dimitri Kabalevsky, himself a renowned Soviet composer, wrote in one of the Soviet Newspapers: "Not a single detail of Shostakovich's Fifth Symphony escaped Bernstein's attention, and at the same time the breadth of the performance was so great as to be rarely heard in performances of this symphony."

Within the hall itself, after the massive concluding chords, the audience was swept out of its seats to shout "Bravo!" and "Bis!" ("Bis" being the European term for "encore"). Bernstein (who had been studying Russian for several weeks) shouted back: *"Bolshoi spasibo!"* ("Many thanks!") "Mr. Bernstein, limp and perspiring from the rigors of the concert and its reception," a correspondent cabled to *The New York Times,* "said he had never had such an ovation." He was called back for bows countless number of times. Bouquets were thrown at him. Finally, to placate this uncontrollable clamor, Bernstein gave two encores with the orchestra: Berlioz' *Roman Carnival Overture* and the Scherzo movement of Prokofiev's Fifth Symphony. He himself announced each of these two numbers in precise, correct Russian, and each number engendered still new outbursts of cheering.

After the audience started to file out of the hall, some of Russia's leading musicians came backstage to shake Bernstein's hand and tell him through an interpreter how deeply his concert had moved them. There was the eminent Soviet violinist, Leonid Kogan; the fine young pianist, Vladimir Ashkanazy; the distinguished Armenian composer, Aram Khatchaturian. Shostakovich was out of town and could not come to this concert; he would hear his symphony played by Bernstein at a later date. Khatchaturian exclaimed that the Philharmonic consisted of "marvelous musicians, many of them surely great artists." Leonid Kogan subsequently wrote in *Pravda* that "in Bernstein's distinguished appearance happily there is to be found great musicality, a genuine temperament, and a high feeling for most different musical styles."

For his third Moscow concert, on August 24, Bernstein planned an unusual program: Stravinsky's Concerto for Piano and Wind Orchestra, never before heard in Russia; the same composer's ballet suite, *The Rite of Spring;* and a provocative work by Charles Ives, also a stranger in Russia, *The Unanswered Question.* For this occasion, Bernstein felt the need of some explanatory comment on his part. In the same charming and informal manner with which he had won the hearts of Americans over television he proceeded through an interpreter to tell the Russian audience something about Ives' theories on music, the pecularities of his style and idiom in *The Unanswered Question.* He also made pertinent remarks about Stravinsky, as the revolutionist who changed the destiny of modern music with *The Rite of Spring,* and as the neo classicist who began looking back to music's past with his piano concerto. "It was not merely a tremendously successful performance," cabled Osgood Caruthers to *The New York Times,* "but also one of the most exciting events in Moscow's recent musical history." The Ives composition made such a strong impression that Bernstein was tempted to ask his audience if it would like to hear it a second time. Encouraged by a resounding cheer, Bernstein repeated his performance.

Bernstein's forty-first birthday on August 25 was not neglected. After the morning rehearsal, Bernstein was given an informal party at the Ukraina Hotel by officials of the orchestra. All day long gifts arrived from lifelong American and new Soviet friends. The director of the Tschaikovsky Conservatory presented him with a beautifully bound score of Prokofiev's opera, *War and Peace*. The librarian of the Moscow Symphony gave him an old photograph of one of the greatest conductors of the late 19th and early 20th centuries, Artur Nikisch—whom Bernstein described as his "musical grandfather," since Nikisch had been one of Koussevitzky's teachers. A young Soviet composer brought him a work written in his honor and constructed from one of the themes from Bernstein's clarinet sonata. "Your piece," remarked Bernstein graciously, "is better than your theme." But what was perhaps the greatest gift of all came that evening at his concert: an overpowering manifestation of affection, appreciation, and homage on the part of the audience that was, as Bernstein said, "truly fabulous and unexpected." Later the same night Soviet officials gave Bernstein a second birthday party.

The Soviet tour then progressed to six equally triumphant performances in Leningrad and four in Kiev. After that came three more concerts in Moscow. Now the darling of all Russia, Bernstein was honored in Moscow by the Soviet Ministry for Culture with a gala party on September 10. Strolling Russian violinists played sentimental folk music. Red Army dancers performed their corybantic routines. A Russian puppet show was a third attraction. After that nine Philharmonic musicians reciprocated with a jam session, and Bernstein with performances at the piano of jazz and boogie-woogie.

At Bernstein's last appearance in the Soviet Union on September 11, he repeated his performance of the Shostakovich Fifth Symphony, this time with the composer in the audience. Shostakovich jumped from his seat, leaped to the stage, and embraced Bernstein as the audience gave them a standing ovation. Twelve young girls brought huge bouquets, distributing the flowers to the men of the orchestra. Backstage, Dimitri Kabalevsky, Prokofiev's widow, and two eminent Soviet conductors (Kirin Kondrashin and Alexander Gauk) were among

146

those waiting to throw their arms around Bernstein in a token of spontaneous affection.

That concert had been the peak of a particularly trying day both for Bernstein and the orchestra. They had been working hard since early morning when a selected audience of Conservatory students and musicians had been invited to the filming of a television program (seen in the United States on October 25) in which Bernstein pointed up the similarities between Soviet and American music with specific references to Shostakovich's Seventh Symphony and Copland's *Billy the Kid.* So exhausted was the orchestra when the night's concert ended that for the first time in their Russian visit they were incapable of playing any encores. Bernstein himself led the men off the stage. Then, since the audience refused to empty the auditorium, he sat down at the piano and played.

Two sentimental episodes further dramatized for Bernstein his first visit to the Soviet Union. After one of his Moscow concerts, a backstage visitor identified himself as Bernstein's uncle, Simeon. When the orchestra departed for Leningrad, Simeon Bernstein went with it. There, on September 3, Lenny arranged to have him speak over the telephone to Boston—the first contact Simeon had had with his brother in forty-nine years.

Less personal, no doubt, but hardly less moving, was Bernstein's meeting with Boris Pasternak. Pasternak is the author of the novel, *Dr. Zhivago,* which was highly critical of life in the Soviet Union. It had been smuggled out of the country and published successfully in Europe and the United States, after which it received the Nobel Prize for Literature. This monumental success earned for Pasternak only severe rebuke from Soviet authors and officials. He was practically in disgrace, scrupulously avoided by his fellow Soviet writers and artists. He was living in comparative obscurity in Peredelino, fifteen miles out of Moscow. Bernstein made it a special point to seek him out. On September 9 he visited Pasternak at his retreat, where they enjoyed a long conversation. "He is the most complete artist I have ever met," said Bernstein of this meeting. "Never have I felt so close to the esthetic truth." Bernstein invited Pasternak to attend his final Moscow concert. This was the author's first public appearance since winning the Nobel Prize. After the concert, Pasternak told Bernstein: "Thank you for taking us into heaven. Now we must return to earth." (Pasternak died at his home in Moscow in late Spring of 1960.)

The New York Philharmonic left the Soviet Union on September 13 to continue its march through Europe. The last European concert took place at the Royal Festival Hall in London on October 10. One day later, conductors, orchestra, and baggage were lifted by KLM across the Atlantic to Washington, D.C., where a pre-season performance had been scheduled for October 12. In a special ceremony, Bernstein was given the key to the city, and on October 13 he was the guest of honor at a luncheon of the National Press Club, where he spoke of some of his Russian experiences. He was unqualifiedly enthusiastic of the people and the reception they gave him, but he was also candid in his criticism of Soviet musicians for their discouragement of all experimental music and their inclination to live comfortably with dead traditions. These remarks caused no little consternation in the Soviet Union, where intelligent, constructive criticism is usually regarded as a form of attack.

On October 15, Bernstein and orchestra were given an official welcome home in New York by Mayor Wagner. At a ceremony in City Hall, the Mayor proclaimed that week as "Philharmonic Week" and presented Bernstein with a gold key to the city.

When the new season of the Philharmonic began in Carnegie Hall on Thursday evening, October 16, signs all along 57th Street proclaimed: "Welcome Home International Heroes." The hall itself was bedecked with flags, banners, and greenery.

When Bernstein came on the stage to play the national anthem, a tumultuous welcome greeted him; and as had been the case in Moscow, the welcome developed into a veritable hurricane after his performance of Shostakovich's Fifth Symphony.

Bernstein and the New York Philharmonic had spoken through that Shostakovich symphony, and other great musical works of art, to the peoples of many different nationalities; people with languages and customs different from their own; people raised in far different political and social backgrounds. But all these different nations had understood the messages of beauty and truth Bernstein was bringing them, because the language of music is universal. "The longer I live," remarked Bernstein about these experiences, "the more I'm convinced that audiences are the same the world over."

CODA

"Whither Lenny?"

Since 1958 Leonard Bernstein has been showered
with honors of all kinds. He has received the Ditson Award,
a citation from the National Music Council, and an award
from the American Symphony Orchestra League for "distinguished" and "outstanding services to American music." He
has been given the medal of the City of New York and the
John H. Finley Medal for service to New York City. His television programs have been honored with the Sylvania and the
George Foster Peabody Awards, probably the highest tributes
coming to a television performer. From Vice President Nixon
he received the award of the Institute of International Education. The Albert Einstein College of Medicine presented him
with the Albert Einstein Commemorative Award in the Arts.
He was the recipient of citations from ASCAP, the Institute of High Fidelity Manufacturers, and the New York Newspaper Guild. And the awards and citations keep coming all
the time.

He is already the most highly acclaimed and most adulated
American musician of his or any other time. Behind him lie

his formidable triumphs as conductor, composer of concert music, composer of musical-comedy scores, pianist, lecturer, teacher, and author. Whatever else he may accomplish in the future, he has already won for himself a place without precedent in the music of this generation.

Truly it has been a career without parallel. In an age of specialization, he had been an eclectic, deservedly likened to the great men of the Renaissance who were so amazingly versatile. In an art where success in any single endeavor usually comes only after the most arduous, painstaking, and intensive background and experience he won fabulous recognition with maiden efforts. He had never conducted a symphony orchestra when he made his fantastic debut with the New York Philharmonic, and with a single performance he won nationwide recognition. He had never written a composition for orchestra when the *Jeremiah Symphony* became one of the most extensively performed new American works of its time, the recipient of the New York Music Critics Circle Award. He had never before written a ballet or a musical comedy when *Fancy Free* and *On the Town* achieved successes of the first magnitude.

He is a concert pianist who never gave a recital in his life. He became the only American-born conductor to direct performances in one of the world's supreme opera theaters, the La Scala in Milan, without ever having appeared before in any other formal opera house. His first book, *The Joy of Music,* published in 1959, became a national best seller. Indeed, as one writer once said of him, Bernstein is a man who always starts at the top.

With his richest, most mature, and most productive years still ahead, where can a man go who not only is already at the top of everything he has tried in music, but who also has tried to do just about everything?

One thing is certain: He will not, he cannot, stand still. His restless energy, insatiable curiosity, immense creative resources, and driving necessity to express himself in all fields of music will never permit him the luxury of resting satisfied with past achievements. No doubt, a berth on the top is a highly comfortable one that encourages relaxation. But for Bernstein even the top must remain a step toward a still higher sphere of achievement.

There are those who still keep on insisting that Bernstein is trying to do too many things at once. Who ever heard—say these skeptics—of one man achieving significance in so many different areas? Such critics refuse to take into account the salient fact that genius is ever a law unto himself, *sui generis*. True genius must create the rules by which he can best function; it does not try to live and create according to rules established by others. Beethoven made his own rules when he created his greatest masterworks while stone deaf; Wagner made his own rules when he spent a quarter of a century creating monumental music dramas for stage techniques, voices, and an orchestra then not able to meet his artistic demands; Delius made his own rules when, blind, he dictated his last works to an amanuensis. And so on, through musical history. None of these masters looked back to precedent for what an inner, irresistible artistic compulsion led them to do.

Leonard Bernstein is a genius, and it is just as ridiculous to indict him for branching out so fruitfully in so many ways as it would have been to condemn Beethoven for trying to write music while deaf, Delius while blind, and Wagner for producing works so far ahead of their time. Like all true genius before him, Bernstein can go only where his overwhelming drives lead him.

Prophecy is a thankless, often futile, always dangerous, task. Nevertheless, from what we already know of Bernstein, both as a man and an artist, we can hardly resist the temptation of foreseeing for him an ever richer, more rewarding and more productive career—and in every conceivable facet of musicmaking. He would not be Leonard Bernstein if he had done otherwise in the past. He would not be Leonard Bernstein if he were to do otherwise in the future.

APPENDIX

I. Works by Leonard Bernstein 157

II. Recordings of Leonard Bernstein's Music . . . 163

III. About Leonard Bernstein 165

Works by Leonard Bernstein

1941–1942

Sonata for Clarinet and Piano. First performance: Boston, April 21, 1942, David Glazer, clarinetist, and Leonard Bernstein, pianist.

1942

Jeremiah Symphony. First performance: Pittsburgh, January 28, 1944, Leonard Bernstein conducting the Pittsburgh Symphony and Jennie Tourel, soloist.

1942–1943

Seven Anniversaries, for solo piano. (1) Aaron Copland; (2) Shirley Bernstein; (3) Serge Koussevitzky; (4) William Schuman; (5) Paul Bowles; (6) Nathalie Koussevitzky; (7) Alfred Eisner. First performance: New York, October 13, 1944, Gordon Manley.

1943

I Hate Music: Song Cycle of Five Kid Songs. (1) My Mother Says Babies Come in Bottles; (2) Jupiter Has Seven Rooms; (3) I Hate Music; (4) A Big Indian and Little Indian; (5) I Just Found Out Today. First Performance: New York, November 13, 1943, Jennie Tourel.

1944

Fancy Free, ballet. First performance: Metropolitan Opera House, New York, April 18, 1944, the Ballet Theater, Leonard Bernstein conducting.

On the Town, musical comedy. Book and lyrics by Betty Comden and Adolph Green, based on an idea by Jerome Robbins. First performance: Adelphi Theater, New York, December 28, 1944. Cast included Sono Osato, Betty Comden, Adolph Green, and Nancy Walker. Staged by George Abbott. Choreography by Jerome Robbins (463 performances). Musical Numbers: I Feel Like I'm Not Out of Bed Yet; New York, New York; Miss Turnstiles; Come Up to My Place; I Get Carried Away; Lonely Town; Do Re Do; I Can Cook; Lucky to Be Me; Sailors on the Town; So Long! I'm Blue; You Got Me; I Understand; Subway to Coney Island; Gabey in the Playground of the Rich; Some Other Time; Coney Island.

1945

Hashkivenu, for four-part mixed voices, cantor, and organ. First performance: Park Avenue Synagogue, New York, May 11, 1945.

1946

Facsimile, ballet. First performance: Broadway Theater, New York, October 24, 1946, the Ballet Theater, Leonard Bernstein conducting.

1947

La Bonne cuisine, song cycle. (1) Plum Pudding; (2) Queues de boeuf; (3) Tavocik guennksis; (4) Civet à toute vitesse. First performance: New York, October 1, 1948, Marion Bell.

1947–1948

Elegy for Mippy I, for horn and piano; *Elegy for Mippy II,* for solo trombone; *Fanfare for Bima,* for trumpet, horn, trom-

158

bone, and tuba; *Rondo for Lifey,* for trumpet and piano; *Waltz for Mippy III,* for tuba and piano. First complete performance: New York, April 8, 1959.

1948

Four Anniversaries, for solo piano. (1) Felicia Montealegre; (2) Johnny Mehegan; (3) David Diamond; (4) Helen Coates. First performance: Cleveland, October 1, 1948, Eudice Podell.

1949

The Age of Anxiety, Symphony No. 2, for piano and orchestra. First performance: Boston, April 8, 1949, the Boston Symphony Orchestra, Serge Koussevitzky conducting and Leonard Bernstein soloist. Music of the symphony was utilized for a ballet of the same name introduced by the New York City Ballet in New York on February 26, 1950.

1950

Incidental music to *Peter Pan,* by James M. Barrie, presented at the Imperial Theater on April 24, 1950, starring Jean Arthur and Boris Karloff. Musical numbers: Who Am I?; My House; Peter, Peter; Never Land; Drink Blood; The Plank.

1952

Trouble in Tahiti, one-act opera. First performance: Festival of Creative Arts, Brandeis University, Waltham, Mass., Leonard Bernstein conducting, June 12, 1952.

Wonderful Town, musical comedy. Book by Joseph Fields and Jerome Chodorov based on the play, *My Sister Eileen* by Joseph Fields and Jerome Chodorov, derived from stories by Ruth McKenny. Lyrics by Adolph Green and Betty Comden. First performance: Winter Garden, February 25, 1953. Cast included Rosalind Russell and Edith Adams. Staged by George Abbott. Dances and musical numbers staged by Donald Saddler

(556 performances). Musical numbers: Christopher Street; Ohio; One Hundred Easy Ways; What a Waste; A Little Bit of Love; Pass the Football; Conversation Piece; A Quiet Girl; Conga; My Darlin' Eileen; Swing; It's Love; Ballet at the Village Vortex; Wrong Note Rag.

1954

Serenade, for violin solo, strings, and percussion. First performance: Venice, Italy, September 12, 1954, Leonard Bernstein conducting, Issac Stern soloist. Music was utilized for ballet, *Serenade for Seven,* first performed at the Spoleto Festival, Italy, July 1959.

Incidental music to *Waterfront,* a motion-picture starring Marlon Brando. Columbia Pictures. Released July 28, 1954.

1955

Incidental music to *The Lark,* by Jean Anouilh, adapted by Lillian Hellman, presented at the Longacre Theater on November 17, 1955, starring Julie Harris.

Prelude, Fanfare and Riffs, for orchestra. First performance: ABC-TV, Omnibus program, October 16, 1955, Leonard Bernstein conducting.

1956

Candide, musical comedy. Book by Lillian Hellman based on Voltaire's satirical novel of the same name. Lyrics by Richard Wilbur, John La Touche, and Dorothy Parker. Cast included Max Adrian, Robert Rouseville, Barbara Cook, and Irra Pettina. Staged by Tyrone Guthrie, with the assistance of Tom Brown (73 performances). Musical numbers: The Best of All Possible Worlds; Oh, Happy We; It Must Be So; Oh, What a Day for a Holiday; It Must Be Me; Glitter and Be Gay; We're Dead, You Know; Pilgrim's Processional; I Am Easily Assimilated;

Quartet—Finale; Eldorado; We Are Women; Bon Voyage; What's the Use?; I've Got Trouble; Make Our Garden Grow.

1957

West Side Story, musical play. Book by Arthur Laurents based on a conception of Jerome Robbins. Lyrics by Stephen Sondheim. Cast included Carol Lawrence, Chita Rivera, and Larry Kert. Directed and with choreography by Jerome Robbins (734 performances). Musical numbers: Prologue; Jet Song; Something's Coming; The Dance at the Gym; Maria; Tonight; America; Cool; One Hand, One Heart; Tonight; The Rumble; I Feel Pretty; Somewhere; Gee, Officer Krupke; A Boy Like That; I Have a Love; Taunting; Finale.

Books

The Joy of Music. New York: Simon and Schuster, 1959. Includes seven Omnibus television scripts.

Recordings of Leonard Bernstein's music

The Age of Anxiety. New York Philharmonic, Leonard Bernstein conducting. Columbia ML-4325.

Candide. Original cast album. Columbia O1-5180.

Fancy Free. New York Philharmonic, Leonard Bernstein conducting, Columbia CL-920; RCA-Victor Symphony, Leonard Bernstein conducting, Camden 196; Ballet Theater Orchestra, Maurice Levine conducting, Capitol P-8320.

Jeremiah Symphony. Pittsburgh Symphony, Leonard Bernstein conducting. Camden 196.

On the Town. Mary Martin and others. Decca 8030; Original cast album, Columbia (in preparation).

Peter Pan. Incidental Music. Mary Martin. Columbia 4312.

Seven Anniversaries. Leonard Bernstein. Camden 214.

Serenade, for violin solo, strings, and percussion. Symphony of the Air, Leonard Bernstein conducting. Columbia ML-5144.

Trouble in Tahiti. Original television cast album. MGM 3646.

West Side Story. Original cast album, Columbia OL-5230; Ballet music, RCA Victor Symphony, Robert Russell Bennett, conducting, Victor LM-2340; The Prince Orchestra, Warner Brothers, B-1240.

Wonderful Town. Original cast album. Columbia OL-5360.

Television Broadcasts

Bernstein on Beethoven. Columbia CL-918.
What Is Jazz? Columbia CL-919.

About Leonard Bernstein

Barrett, Marvin: "The Five Careers of Leonard Bernstein." *Reader's Digest,* May 1960.

Close-Up: "Busy Time for a Young Maestro." *Life,* January 7, 1957.

Harris, Eleanor: "The Happy Genius." *Saturday Evening Post,* June 16, 1956.

Lindsay, David R.: "The Remarkable, Musical Mr. Bernstein." *Coronet,* December 1956.

Moor, Paul: "Leonard Bernstein: Ceiling Unlimited." *Harper's,* February 1948.

Morton, Frederic: "The Exceptional Musician: Leonard Bernstein." *Holiday,* October 1959.

Rice, Robert: "The Pervasive Musician." A two-part Profile, *The New Yorker,* January 11–18, 1958.

Richmond, John: "Portrait of a Genius." *Tomorrow,* May 1945.

Roddy, Joseph: "Who Lives at Carnegie Hall?" *High Fidelity Magazine,* February 1959.

Schonberg, Harold C.: "New Job for the Protean Mr. Bernstein." *The New York Times Magazine,* December 22, 1957.

Schonberg, Harold C.: "What Bernstein Is Doing to the Philharmonic. *Harper's,* May 1959.

Schubart, Mark A.: "A Triple Note Man of the Music World." *The New York Times Magazine,* January 28, 1945.

Time Magazine Cover Story: "Wunderkind." *Time,* February 4, 1957.

Index

Abbott, George, 75, 76, 110, 111, 158, 159
Accompanist, Bernstein as, 24, 47
Adams, Edith, 159
Adelphi Theater, 76
Adrian, Max, 160
Advocate, The, 24
Age of Anxiety, The, 102–104, 142, 159, 163
All in One, 108
Amber, Lenny, 49
Amberg, George, 72
American Ballet Theater, 71
American Exposition in Russia, 142
American Federation of Musicians, 44, 91
American National Theater and Academy, 139
Anouilh, Jean, 160
Apollo Rooms, 129
Argentina, appearances in, 140
Arrau, Claudio, 105
Arthur, Jean, 159
Ashkanazy, Vladimir, 144
Aston, Frank, 126
Athletics, success in, 15
Atkinson, Brooks, 76, 111, 121, 125
Auden, W. H., 102
Austria, appearances in, 90, 142

Awards received by Bernstein, 70, 73, 95, 104, 110, 151

Bach, 63, 64, 99
  talk on, 115–116, 122
Baehr, Johann, 60
Ballet, 72
Ballet music, for *Facsimile,* 101–102
  for *Fancy Free,* 71–73
  for *Serenade for Seven,* 112
Ballet Theater, 71, 101
Bankhead, Tallulah, 42–43
Barber, Samuel, 88, 140, 142, 143
Barbirolli, John, 132
Bartók, Béla, 87, 93, 100
Baton, use of, 60–61
Beecham, Sir Thomas, 88
Beethoven, 7, 37, 63, 64, 99, 135, 142, 153
  talk on, 114–115, 164
Belgium, appearances in, 90
Bell, Marion, 158
Bennett, Robert Russell, 163
Berg, Alban, 87
Bergmann, Carl, 130–131
Berkshire Music Center, 38–43, 46, 51, 106
Berkshire Symphonic Festival, 37, 51, 93

Berlin, Irving, 32
Berlioz, Hector, 61, 136, 144
Bernstein, Alexander Serge, 117
  Burton, 9
  Jamie, 117
  Jennie, 9
  Samuel Joseph, 7–9, 12, 17, 20–21,
    22, 31, 45, 47, 55
  Shirley, 9, 11, 14, 18, 50, 73, 106,
    157
  Simeon, 147
Biancolli, Louis, 112
Blackwood, Easley, 135
Blitzstein, Marc, 25–27, 30, 87
Bloch, Ernest, 68
Bolivia, appearances in, 139
Bonne cuisine, La, 102, 158
Boston, Bernstein family in, 9
  On the Town in, 75
Boston Latin School, 15, 21
Boston Opera House, 73
Boston Pops Orchestra, 68
Boston Public School Orchestra,
    15–16
Boston Symphony, 19, 28, 37, 38, 42,
    68, 69, 87, 89, 93–94, 103, 122
  difficulties with union, 44–45
Bowles, Paul, 157
Brahms, 35, 63, 64, 99, 104
Brandeis University, 107, 108, 113
Brando, Marlon, 123, 160
Brazil, appearances in, 140
Britten, Benjamin, 88
Brookline, Massachusetts, 46
Brown, Tom, 160
Bruckner, 63

Caesar, Irving, 48
Callas, Maria, 93
Camp, summer, 15, 17, 25

Candide, 120–122, 160, 163
Carnegie Hall, debut in, 1–5, 55–58,
    152
Carnegie Hall Playhouse, 77
Caruthers, Osgood, 145
Central America, appearances in,
    139–141
Chasins, Abram, 113
Chávez, Carlos, 44, 88
Cherubini, 93
Chicago, appearances in, 68
Childhood days, 9–18
Chile, appearances in, 140
Chodorov, Jerome, 109, 159
Cincinnati Symphony, 89
Clurman, Harold, 32
Coates, Helen, 13, 21, 23, 52, 79,
    117, 159
Cohn, Felicia Montealegre, 105, 159
Coleman, Robert, 109, 121, 126
Colombia, appearances in, 139
Colonne, Edouard, 131
Comden, Betty, 31, 48, 74–75, 108,
    158, 159
Compositions, 157–161
  early, 14, 18, 23, 30, 45–46, 50
  first ballet score, 71–73 (see also
    Ballet music)
  first opera, 107, 159, 163
  first symphony, 50, 69–71, 88, 89,
    93, 152, 157, 163
  later, 67–77, 101–102, 111–112
  musical comedies (see Musical
    comedies)
  second symphony, 102–104, 142,
    159, 163
Concert appearances (see Conduct-
    ing)
Concertgebouw Orchestra, 93, 132

168

Conducting, debut in, 1–5, 55–58, 152
  first experiences with, 25, 28–29, 36, 49
  genius of Bernstein, 96–100
  guest appearances, 68, 87, 88–90
  on tours, 96, 139–149
Conductors, function of, 59–66
Contest, for music information, 18
  for symphonic work, 50
Conway, Harold, 126
Cook, Barbara, 160
Copland, Aaron, 23, 24, 27, 30, 32, 35, 39, 45, 49, 73, 88, 94, 100, 140, 142, 147, 157
Cradle Will Rock, The, 25–27, 87
Criticisms, musical, written by Bernstein, 24
Curtis Institute of Music, 34–37, 42
Curtis Institute Orchestra, 36
Czech Philharmonic, 88

Daily Express, 122, 126
Daily Mail, 126
Daily News, 58
Daily Sketch, 126
Damrosch, Leopold, 131
  Walter, 131, 132
Debut, at Carnegie Hall, 1–5, 55–58, 152
Delius, 153
Denby, Edwin, 72
De Witt Clinton Adult Center, 77
Diamond, David, 94, 142, 159
Dorsey, Tommy, 78
Downes, Olin, 57
Draper, Paul, 108
Duke, Vernon, 46, 87

Ecuador, appearances in, 140
Education (*see* Schools)

Eisenhower, Dwight, 139, 141
Eisfeld, Theodore, 130
Eisner, Alfred, 157
Elegy for Mippy I, 158
Elegy for Mippy II, 158
Employment, 21, 22, 47–49
England, appearances in, 90, 92, 121, 142, 148
Ernst, Fritz, 143
Etienne, D., 130
Europe, tour of, 141–143

Facsimile, 101–102, 107, 158
Fancy Free, 71–73, 102, 152, 158, 163
Fanfare for Bima, 158
Festival of Creative Arts, at Brandeis, 107
Fields, Joseph, 109, 159
Films, piano accompaniments to, 24
Fine, Irving, 24
Finland, appearances in, 142
Florida, vacation in, 18
Foote, 135
Four Anniversaries, 159
France, appearances in, 90, 142
Frederick R. Mann Auditorium, 96, 122

Gaburo, Kenneth, 135
Garfield, John, 33
Garrett, Betty, 77
Gauk, Alexander, 146
Gebhard, Heinrich, 13, 23, 28, 30
Germany, appearances in, 90, 93, 142
Gershwin, George, 25, 48, 79, 88, 95, 140, 142
Gilbert, 135
Gilbert and Sullivan, 17, 31

Girl with Two Left Feet, The, 32
Glazer, David, 46, 157
Gradenwitz, Peter, 89
Greece, appearances in, 141
Green, Adolph, 31, 48, 74–75, 81,
    108, 158, 159
Group Theater, 32
Guarnieri, Camargo, 49
Guthrie, Tyrone, 160

Handel, 7, 99, 135
Harper's Bazaar, 78
Harris, Roy, 30, 88, 140
Harrison, Jay, 112
Harvard, 22–30
Haskivenu, 158
Hawkins, Coleman, 48
Haydn, 63, 99
Heifetz, 20
Hellman, Lillian, 120, 160
Herald Tribune, 57, 68, 72, 77, 112,
    126
Hill, Edward Burlingame, 23
Hill, U. C., 130
Hindemith, Paul, 40, 45, 63, 88, 94
Hines, Earl, 48
Holland, appearances in, 90, 93, 142
Holland Music Festival, 93
Holliday, Judy, 32
Hospital, composing in, 74
Houseman, John, 26
Houston Symphony, 89
Huneker, James Gibbons, 129
Hungary, appearances in, 93

I Hate Music: Five Kid Songs, 50,
    52, 53, 157
Information Please program, 79, 80
Institute of Modern Art, in Boston,
    45, 46

International Festival in Prague, 88,
    90
International Program for Cultural
    Presentations, 139, 141
Israel Philharmonic, 94–96, 122
Italy, appearances in, 93, 112, 142
Ives, Charles, 94, 135, 136, 142, 145

Jeremiah Symphony, 50, 69–71, 88,
    89, 93, 152, 157, 163
Journal-American, 125
Joy of Music, The, 79, 152, 161

Kabalevsky, Dimitri, 144, 146
Kalliwoda, Johann Wenzel, 130
Karloff, Boris, 159
Kazan, Elia, 33
Keiser, David, 127
Kelly, Gene, 77
Kerr, Walter, 77, 126
Kert, Larry, 161
Khatchaturian, Aram, 144, 145
Klesmer, 8
Kogan, Leonid, 144, 145
Kolodin, Irving, 108
Kondrashin, Kirin, 146
Koussevitzky, Nathalie, 157
    Serge, 19, 20, 25, 37–42, 46, 47,
    51, 57, 69, 73, 76, 84, 88, 93–94,
    96, 103, 105, 157, 159

La Guardia, Fiorello, 87
Lambert, Constant, 42
Lamentation, 50
Lark, The, incidental music to, 160
La Scala opera house, 93, 152
La Touche, John, 120, 160
Laurents, Arthur, 123, 161
Lawrence, Carol, 161
Lebanon, appearances in, 142

Lenox, Massachusetts, 37, 51
Levine, Maurice, 163
Lewisohn Stadium, 68, 87
Lipkin, Seymour, 142
List, Eugene, 88
Liszt, Franz, 61, 99, 130
Los Angeles, appearances in, 68
Lully, Jean-Baptiste, 60
Luxembourg, appearances in, 142

McClain, John, 125
MacDowell, 135
McKenney, Ruth, 108, 159
Mahler, Gustav, 63, 93, 99, 132, 135
Malipiero, 29
Manley, Gordon, 73
Marriage, 105–106
Martin, John, 72
Martin, Mary, 163
Martin Beck Theater, 121
Massachusetts State Orchestra, 24
Mehegan, Johnny, 159
Mendelberg, Willem, 93, 132
Mendelssohn, Felix, 61
Menotti, Gian-Carlo, 112
Merriman, Nan, 71
Merritt, Arthur Tillman, 23
Messiaen, Olivier, 94
Mexico, appearances in, 139
    vacations in, 105, 106–107
Milhaud, 88
Miller, Ann, 77
Milstein, Nathan, 90
Minneapolis Symphony, 89
Mirror, New York, 110, 121
Mishkan Tefila, Temple, 10, 15,
    106
Mitropoulos, Dimitri, 28–29, 30,
    34–35, 64, 126–127, 132, 139
Modern Music, 24, 70

Montreal Symphony, 68
Moscow Symphony, 146
Mozart, 63, 88, 99, 142, 143
    talk on, 116
Munch, Charles, 88, 94, 107
Music Publishers Holding Corporation, 48
Musical comedies: *Candide,* 120–122
    On the Town, 75–77
    West Side Story, 123–126
    Wonderful Town, 109–111
    My Sister Eileen, 108–109

National Symphony, 132
NBC Symphony, 89
New York City Ballet, 104
New York City Symphony, 87–88,
    91–92
New York Philharmonic, 36, 87, 93,
    122, 126–128
    Bernstein as music director, 51–
    52, 127–128, 133–138
    debut with, 1–5, 55–58, 152
    history of, 129–132
    tours with, 139–149
New York Symphony Society, 132
New York Times, The, 57, 72, 73,
    76, 78, 89, 104, 144, 145
New Yorker, 109
Nichols, Lewis, 76
Nikisch, Artur, 146
Nixon, Richard, 142, 151
North, Alex, 87
Norway, appearances in, 142

Odets, Clifford, 33
Omnibus programs, 114, 122
On the Town, 75–77, 152, 163
Onions, Oliver, 79
Onota, Camp, 15, 17, 25

Opera: *Trouble in Tahiti,* 107, 159, 163

Oppenheim, David, 49

Osato, Sono, 75, 158

Palestine Philharmonic, 89, 94–96

Panama Canal, cruise through, 18

Paramount Pictures, 79

Parker, Dorothy, 120, 160

Parties, entertaining at, 15, 16, 18, 32, 36

Pasternak, Boris, 147

Pergolesi, 135

Personality of Bernstein, 78–83, 117–119

Peter Pan, incidental music to, 159, 163

Petrillo, James Caesar, 44

Pettina, Irra, 160

Philadelphia, music school in, 34–37

Piano, first experiences with, 10–11 lessons on, 12–15, 36

Piatigorsky, Gregor, 96

Piston, Walter, 23, 30, 142

Pittsburgh Symphony, 68–69, 87, 103

Poland, appearances in, 142

Prelude, Fanfare and Riffs, 160

Preview Concerts, 135–136

Prokofiev, 100, 144, 145

Pulitzer, Joseph, 132

Purcell, 88

Rachmaninoff, Serge, 18, 20, 84

Radio programs, 136

Ravel G major Piano Concerto, 23, 68, 90, 139

Ravinia Park, 68

Recipes, set to music, 102

Recordings, 71, 73, 122, 134, 137, 163

Reiner, Fritz, 34–37, 40, 47

Resnick, Jennie, 9

Reviews, of *Age of Anxiety,* 104
  of *Candide,* 121
  of conducting debut, 57–58
  of European tour, 143
  of *Fancy Free,* 72
  of *Jeremiah Symphony,* 70
  of *On the Town,* 76
  of Palestine performance, 89–90
  of preview concerts, 136
  of Russian tour, 144, 145
  of *Serenade,* 112
  of *Seven Anniversaries,* 73
  of television appearances, 116
  of *Trouble in Tahiti,* 108
  of *West Side Story,* 125–126
  of *Wonderful Town,* 109–110, 111
  written by Bernstein, 24

Rivera, Chita, 161

Robbins, Jerome, 71, 75, 101, 104, 112, 123, 158, 161

Rochester Philharmonic, 89

Rodzinski, Artur, 51, 54, 57, 132

Rondo for Lifey, 159

Rouseville, Robert, 160

Rózsa, Miklós, 54

Rubinstein, Artur, 96

Russell, Rosalind, 109, 111, 159

Russia, Bernstein's father in, 8
  Koussevitzky in, 38
  tour of, 142, 143–149

Saddler, Donald, 159

Safonov, Vassily, 131, 132

St. Louis Symphony, 71, 87, 89

Saturday Review, 108

Saville Theater, 121
Schippers, Thomas, 142
Schoenberg, Arnold, 104
Schools, at Berkshire Music Center, 38–43
    Boston Latin School, 15, 21
    Curtis Institute of Music, 34–37, 42
    early education in, 15, 21–22, 23–30
    Harvard, 22–30
Schuman, William, 30, 73, 88, 135, 140, 157
Schumann, Robert, 2, 7, 29, 54, 93, 99, 128
Serenade, 111–112, 160, 163
Serenade for Seven, 112
Seven Anniversaries, 73, 157, 163
Shapero, Harold, 94
Shostakovich, 100, 122, 128, 144, 146, 147, 149
Sight reading of scores, 35, 37
Sinatra, Frank, 77, 78
Sitwell, Sacheverell, 42
Smith, Oliver, 71
Smith, Warren Story, 70
Sonata for clarinet and piano, 46, 49, 157
Sondheim, Stephen, 125, 161
South America, appearances in, 139–141
    Toscanini in, 4
Spohr, Louis, 60
Spoleto Festival in Italy, 112
Sports, success in, 15
Starr, Herman, 48
Stern, Isaac, 96, 112, 160
Stokowski, Leopold, 87
Stransky, Josef, 132

Strauss, Johann, 7
    Richard, 2, 54, 128, 131
Stravinsky, Igor, 19, 24, 63, 88, 94, 100, 145
Sullivan, Gilbert and, 17, 31
Sweden, appearances in, 142
Switzerland, appearances in, 142
Symphonies: *Age of Anxiety*, 102–104, 142, 159, 163
    Jeremiah Symphony, 50, 69–71, 88, 89, 93, 152, 157, 163
Symphony Hall, 18, 19, 93

Tanglewood, 7, 37–43, 46, 88, 106, 108, 122, 134
Taubman, Howard, 104, 108, 116, 128, 136
Teaching of music, 47, 113–117
Television appearances, 113–117, 136, 164
Temple Mishkan Tefila, 10, 15, 106
Thomas, Theodore, 131
Thompson, John, 121, 126
Thompson, Randall, 36
Thomson, Virgil, 49, 68, 70, 99
Time magazine, 76
Timm, H. C., 130
Toscanini, Arturo, 4, 20, 89, 132, 138
Tourel, Jennie, 52, 53–54, 69, 157
Tours, conducting, 96, 139–149
Town Hall, appearances in, 49, 53
Trouble in Tahiti, 107, 159, 163
Tschaikovsky, 79
Tschaikovsky Conservatory, 143, 145
Turkey, appearances in, 142
Turner, Charles, 140

Ukraina Hotel, 145
Union, Musicians, 32, 44–45, 91
Uruguay, appearances in, 140

Vancouver Symphony, 87
Vanguard, The, 32
Venezuela, appearances in, 139, 140
Vengerova, Isabella, 36
Venice Festival in Italy, 112
Voltaire, 120, 160

Wagner, Richard, 2, 54, 62, 63, 130, 153
Walker, Nancy, 75, 158
Walter, Bruno, 2, 54, 55, 64
Waltham, Massachusetts, 107
Waltz for Mippy III, 159
War years, activity during, 45, 47, 51
Warner Brothers, 79
Waterfront, incidental music to, 123, 160

Weber, Karl Maria von, 130
Weingartner, Felix, 131
Welles, Orson, 26
West Side Story, 123–126, 161, 163
Wilbur, Richard, 120, 160
Williams, Tennessee, 108
Wilson, Cecil, 126
Winter Garden, 123
WNYC, performances on, 49
Wonderful Town, 109–111, 159, 163
Works of Bernstein (*see* Compositions)
World-Telegram, 112, 126

Youmans, Vincent, 48
Yugoslavia, appearances in, 142

Zirato, Bruno, 54, 55